John Ruskin

Time And Tide by Weare and Tyne

25 Letters to a Working Man of Sunderland on the Laws of Work. Fourth Edition

John Ruskin

Time And Tide by Weare and Tyne
25 Letters to a Working Man of Sunderland on the Laws of Work. Fourth Edition

ISBN/EAN: 9783744744508

Printed in Europe, USA, Canada, Australia, Japan

Cover: Foto ©ninafisch / pixelio.de

More available books at **www.hansebooks.com**

TIME AND TIDE.

TIME AND TIDE

BY

WEARE AND TYNE.

TWENTY-FIVE LETTERS TO
A WORKING MAN OF SUNDERLAND
ON
THE LAWS OF WORK.

By JOHN RUSKIN,
HONORARY STUDENT OF CHRISTCHURCH, AND HONORARY FELLOW OF
CORPUS CHRISTI COLLEGE, OXFORD.

FOURTH EDITION.

GEORGE ALLEN,
SUNNYSIDE, ORPINGTON,
AND
8, BELL YARD, TEMPLE BAR, LONDON,
1891.

[*All rights reserved.*]

Printed by Hazell, Watson, & Viney, Ld., London and Aylesbury.

CONTENTS.

	PAGE
PREFACE	ix

LETTER
I. CO-OPERATION 1
　　The two kinds of Co-operation.—In its highest sense it is not yet thought of.

II. CONTENTMENT 7
　　Co-operation, as hitherto understood, is perhaps not expedient.

III. LEGISLATION 14
　　Of True Legislation.—That every Man may be a Law to himself.

IV. EXPENDITURE 21
　　The Expenses for Art and for War.

V. ENTERTAINMENT 25
　　The Corruption of Modern Pleasure.— (Covent Garden Pantomime.)

VI. DEXTERITY 33
　　The Corruption of Modern Pleasure.—(The Japanese Jugglers.)

VII. FESTIVITY 37
　　Of the Various Expressions of National Festivity.

VIII. THINGS WRITTEN 41
　　The Four possible Theories respecting the Authority of the Bible.

CONTENTS.

LETTER		PAGE
IX.	THANKSGIVING	49

    The Use of Music and Dancing under the Jewish Theocracy, compared with their Use by the Modern French.

| X. | WHEAT-SIFTING | 60 |

    The Meaning, and Actual Operation, of Satanic or Demoniacal Influence.

| XI. | THE GOLDEN BOUGH | 71 |

    The Satanic Power is mainly Twofold: the Power of causing Falsehood and the Power of causing Pain. The Resistance is by Law of Honour and Law of Delight.

| XII. | DICTATORSHIP | 76 |

    The Necessity of Imperative Law to the Prosperity of States.

| XIII. | EPISCOPACY AND DUKEDOM | 85 |

    The Proper Offices of the Bishop and Duke; or, "Overseer" and "Leader."

| XIV. | TRADE-WARRANT | 95 |

    The First Group of Essential Laws.—Against Theft by False Work, and by Bankruptcy.—Necessary Publicity of Accounts.

| XV. | PER-CENTAGE | 101 |

    The Nature of Theft by Unjust Profits.—Crime can finally be arrested only by Education.

| XVI. | EDUCATION | 110 |

    Of Public Education irrespective of Class-distinction. It consists essentially in giving Habits of Mercy, and Habits of Truth. (*Gentleness and Justice.*)

CONTENTS.

LETTER		PAGE
XVII.	DIFFICULTIES	123
	The Relations of Education to Position in Life.	
XVIII.	HUMILITY	128
	The harmful Effects of Servile Employments. The possible Practice and Exhibition of sincere Humility by Religious Persons.	
XIX.	BROKEN REEDS	136
	The General Pressure of Excessive and Improper Work, in English Life.	
XX.	ROSE-GARDENS	146
	Of Improvidence in Marriage in the Middle Classes; and of the advisable Restrictions of it.	
XXI.	GENTILLESSE	156
	Of the Dignity of the Four Fine Arts; and of the Proper System of Retail Trade.	
XXII.	THE MASTER	164
	Of the normal Position and Duties of the Upper Classes. General Statement of the Land Question.	
XXIII.	LANDMARKS	174
	Of the Just Tenure of Lands; and the Proper Functions of high Public Officers.	
XXIV.	THE ROD AND HONEYCOMB	189
	The Office of the Soldier.	
XXV.	HYSSOP	202
	Of inevitable Distinction of Rank, and necessary Submission to Authority. The Meaning of Pure-Heartedness. Conclusion.	

APPENDICES.

APPENDIX		PAGE
I.	Expenditure on Science and Art . . .	217
II.	Legislation of Frederick the Great . . .	219
III.	Effect of Modern Entertainments on the Mind of Youth.	224
IV.	Drunkenness as the Cause of Crime . . .	225
V.	Abuse of Food	228
VI.	Regulations of Trade	230
VII.	Letter to the Editor of the *Pall Mall Gazette* .	233

PREFACE.

THE following Letters were written to Mr. Thomas Dixon, a working cork-cutter of Sunderland, during the agitation for Reform in the spring of the present year. They contain, in the plainest terms I could use, the substance of what I then desired to say to our English workmen, which was briefly this:—" The reform you desire may give you more influence in Parliament; but your influence there will of course be useless to you, —perhaps worse than useless,—until you have wisely made up your minds what you wish Parliament to do for you ; and when you *have* made up your minds about that, you will find, not only that you can do it for yourselves, without the intervention of Parliament; but that eventually nobody *but* yourselves can do it. And to help you, as far as one of your old friends may, in so making up your minds, such and such things are what it seems to me you should ask for, and, moreover, strive for with your heart and might."

The letters now published relate only to one division of the laws which I desired to recommend to the consideration of our operatives,—those, namely, bearing upon honesty of work, and honesty of exchange. I hope in the course of next year that I may be able to complete the second part of the series, [I could not; but 'Fors Clavigera' is now (1872) answering the same end:] which will relate to the possible comforts and wholesome laws, of familiar household life, and the share which a labouring nation may attain in the skill, and the treasures, of the higher arts.

The letters are republished as they were

written, with, here and there, correction of a phrase, and omission of one or two passages of merely personal or temporary interest; the headings only are added, in order to give the reader some clue to the general aim of necessarily desultory discussion; and the portions of Mr. Dixon's letters in reply, referred to in the text, are added in the Appendix, and will be found well deserving of attention.

DENMARK HILL,
December 14, 1867.

TIME AND TIDE,

BY

WEARE AND TYNE.

LETTER I.

The two kinds of Co-operation.—In its highest sense it is not yet thought of.

DENMARK HILL, *February* 4, 1867.

MY DEAR FRIEND,

1. You have now everything I have yet published on political economy; but there are several points in these books of mine which I intended to add notes to, and it seems little likely I shall get that soon done. So I think the best way of making up for the want of these is to write you a few simple letters, which you can read to other people, or send to be printed, if you like, in any of your journals where you think they may be useful.

I especially want you, for one thing, to understand the sense in which the word "co-operation" is used in my books. You will find I am always pleading for it; and yet I don't at all mean the co-operation of partnership (as opposed to the system of wages) which is now so gradually extending itself among our great firms. I am glad to see it doing so, yet not altogether glad: for none of you who are engaged in the immediate struggle between the system of co-operation and the system of mastership know how much the dispute involves; and none of us know the results to which it may finally lead. For the alternative is not, in reality, only between two modes of conducting business—it is between two different states of society. It is not the question whether an amount of wages, no greater in the end than that at present received by the men, may be paid to them in a way which shall give them share in the risks and interest in the prosperity of the business. The question is, really, whether the profits which are at present taken, as his own right, by the person whose capital, or energy, or ingenuity, has made him head of the firm, are not in some proportion to be divided among the subordinates of it.

2. I do not wish, for the moment, to enter into any inquiry as to the just claims of capital, or as to the proportions in which profits ought to be, or are in actually existing firms, divided. I merely take the one assured and essential condition, that a somewhat larger income will be in co-operative firms secured to the subordinates, by the diminution of the income of the chief. And the general tendency of such a system is to increase the facilities of advancement among the subordinates; to stimulate their ambition; to enable them to lay by, if they are provident, more ample and more early provision for declining years; and to form in the end a vast class of persons wholly different from the existing operative:—members of society, possessing each a moderate competence; able to procure, therefore, not indeed many of the luxuries, but all the comforts of life; and to devote some leisure to the attainments of liberal education, and to the other objects of free life. On the other hand, by the exact sum which is divided among them, more than their present wages, the fortune

of the man who, under the present system, takes all the profits of the business, will be diminished; and the acquirement of large private fortune by regular means, and all the conditions of life belonging to such fortune, will be rendered impossible in the mercantile community.

3. Now, the magnitude of the social change hereby involved, and the consequent differences in the moral relations between individuals, have not as yet been thought of,—much less estimated,—by any of your writers on commercial subjects; and it is because I do not yet feel able to grapple with them that I have left untouched, in the books I send you, the question of co-operative labour. When I use the word "co-operation," it is not meant to refer to these new constitutions of firms at all. I use the word in a far wider sense, as opposed, not to masterhood, but to *competition*. I do not mean, for instance, by co-operation, that all the master bakers in a town are to give a share of their profits to the men who go out with the bread; but that the masters are not to try to undersell each other, nor seek each to get the other's business, but are all

to form one society, selling to the public under a common law of severe penalty for unjust dealing, and at an established price. I do not mean that all bankers' clerks should be partners in the bank; but I do mean that all bankers should be members of a great national body, answerable as a society for all deposits; and that the private business of speculating with other people's money should take another name than that of "banking." And, for final instance, I mean by "co-operation" not only fellowships between trading *firms*, but between trading *nations;* so that it shall no more be thought (as it is now, with ludicrous and vain selfishness) an advantage for one nation to undersell another ; and take its occupation away from it; but that the primal and eternal law of vital commerce shall be of all men understood—namely, that every nation is fitted by its character, and the nature of its territories, for some particular employments or manufactures; and that it is the true interest of every other nation to encourage it in such speciality, and by no means to interfere with, but in all ways forward and protect, its efforts, ceasing all rivalship with it, so soon as it is strong enough to occupy its proper place. You see, therefore, that the idea of co-operation, in the sense in which I employ it, has hardly yet entered into the minds of political inquirers; and I will not pursue it at present; but return to that system which is beginning to obtain credence and practice among us. This, however, must be in a following letter.

LETTER II.

Co-operation, as hitherto understood, is perhaps not expedient.

February 4, 1867.

4. LIMITING the inquiry, then, for the present, as proposed in the close of my last letter, to the form of co-operation which is now upon its trial in practice, I would beg of you to observe that the points at issue, in the comparison of this system with that of mastership, are by no means hitherto frankly stated; still less can they as yet be fairly brought to test. For all mastership is not alike in principle; there are just and unjust masterships; and while, on the one hand, there can be no question but that co-operation is better than unjust and tyrannous mastership, there is very great room for doubt whether it be better than a just and benignant mastership.

5. At present you—every one of you— speak, and act, as if there were only one

alternative; namely, between a system in which profits shall be divided in due proportion among all; and the present one, in which the workman is paid the least wages he will take, under the pressure of competition in the labour-market. But an intermediate method is conceivable; a method which appears to me more prudent, and in its ultimate results more just, than the co-operative one. An arrangement may be supposed, and I have good hope also may one day be effected, by which every subordinate shall be paid sufficient and regular wages, according to his rank; by which due provision shall be made out of the profits of the business for sick and superannuated workers; and by which the master, *being held responsible, as a minor king or governor, for the conduct as well as the comfort of all those under his rule,* shall, on that condition, be permitted to retain to his own use the surplus profits of the business which the fact of his being its master may be assumed to prove that he has organised by superior intellect and energy. And I think this principle of regular wage-paying, whether it be in the abstract more just, or not, is at all events the more prudent; for this reason mainly, that in spite of all the cant which is continually talked by cruel, foolish, or designing persons about "the duty of remaining content in the position in which Providence has placed you," there is a root of the very deepest and holiest truth in the saying, which gives to it such power as it still retains, even uttered by unkind and unwise lips, and received into doubtful and embittered hearts.

6. If, indeed, no effort be made to discover, in the course of their early training, for what services the youths of a nation are individually qualified; nor any care taken to place those who have unquestionably proved their fitness for certain functions, in the offices they could best fulfil,—then, to call the confused wreck of social order and life brought about by malicious collision and competition, an arrangement of Providence, is quite one of the most insolent and wicked ways in which it is possible to take the name of God in vain. But if, at the proper time, some earnest effort be made to place youths, according to their capacities, in the occupations for which they are fitted, I think the system of organisation will be finally found the best, which gives the least encouragement

to thoughts of any great future advance in social life.

7. The healthy sense of progress, which is necessary to the strength and happiness of men, does not consist in the anxiety of a struggle to attain higher place, or rank, but in gradually perfecting the manner, and accomplishing the ends, of the life which we have chosen, or which circumstances have determined for us. Thus, I think the object of a workman's ambition should not be to become a master; but to attain daily more subtle and exemplary skill in his own craft, to save from his wages enough to enrich and complete his home gradually with more delicate and substantial comforts; and to lay by such store as shall be sufficient for the happy maintenance of his old age (rendering him independent of the help provided for the sick and indigent by the arrangement pre-supposed), and sufficient also for the starting of his children in a rank of life equal to his own. If his wages are not enough to enable him to do this, they are unjustly low; if they are once raised to this adequate standard, I do not think that by the possible increase of his gains under

contingencies of trade, or by divisions of profits with his master, he should be enticed into feverish hope of an entire change of condition; and as an almost necessary consequence, pass his days in an anxious discontent with immediate circumstances, and a comfortless scorn of his daily life, for which no subsequent success could indemnify him. And I am the more confident in this belief, because, even supposing a gradual rise in social rank possible for all well-conducted persons, my experience does not lead me to think the elevation itself, when attained, would be conducive to their happiness.

8. The grounds of this opinion I will give you in a future letter; in the present one, I must pass to a more important point—namely, that if this stability of condition be indeed desirable for those in whom existing circumstances might seem to justify discontent, much more must it be good and desirable for those who already possess everything which can be conceived necessary to happiness. It is the merest insolence of selfishness to preach contentment to a labourer who gets thirty shillings a week, while we suppose an active and plotting

covetousness to be meritorious in a man who has three thousand a year. In this, as in all other points of mental discipline, it is the duty of the upper classes to set an example to the lower; and to recommend and justify the restraint of the ambition of their inferiors, chiefly by severe and timely limitation of their own. And, without at present inquiring into the greater or less convenience of the possible methods of accomplishing such an object, (every detail in suggestions of this kind necessarily furnishing separate matter of dispute,) I will merely state my long-fixed conviction, that one of the most important conditions of a healthful system of social economy, would be the restraint of the properties and incomes of the upper classes within certain fixed limits. The temptation to use every energy in the accumulation of wealth being thus removed, another, and a higher ideal of the duties of advanced life would be necessarily created in the national mind; by withdrawal of those who had attained the prescribed limits of wealth from commercial competition, earlier worldly success, and earlier marriage, with all its beneficent moral results, would become possible to the young; while the older men of active intellect, whose sagacity is now lost or warped in the furtherance of their own meanest interests, would be induced unselfishly to occupy themselves in the superintendence of public institutions, or furtherance of public advantage.

And out of this class it would be found natural and prudent always to choose the members of the legislative body of the Commons; and to attach to the order also some peculiar honours, in the possession of which such complacency would be felt as would more than replace the unworthy satisfaction of being supposed richer than others, which to many men is the principal charm of their wealth. And although no law of this purport would ever be imposed on themselves by the actual upper classes, there is no hindrance to its being gradually brought into force from beneath, without any violent or impatient proceedings; and this I will endeavour to show you in my next letter.

LETTER III.

Of True Legislation. That every Man may be a Law to himself.

February 17, 1867.

9. NO, I have not been much worse in health; but I was asked by a friend to look over some work in which you will all be deeply interested one day, so that I could not write again till now. I was the more sorry, because there were several things I wished to note in your last letter; one especially leads me directly to what I in any case was desirous of urging upon you. You say, "In vol. 6th of ' Frederick the Great ' I find a great deal that I feel quite certain, if our Queen or Government could make law, thousands of our English workmen would hail with a shout of joy and gladness." I do not remember to what you especially allude, but whatever the rules you speak of may be, unless there be anything in

them contrary to the rights of present English property, why should you care whether the Government makes them law or not? Can you not, you thousands of English workmen, simply make them a law to yourselves, by practising them?

It is now some five or six years since I first had occasion to speak to the members of the London Working Men's College on the subject of Reform, and the substance of what I said to them was this: "You are all agape, my friends, for this mighty privilege of having your opinions represented in Parliament. The concession might be desirable,—at all events courteous,—if only it were quite certain you had got any opinions to represent. But have you? Are you agreed on any single thing you systematically want? Less work and more wages, of course; but how much lessening of work do you suppose is possible? Do you think the time will ever come for everybody to have *no* work and *all* wages? Or have you yet taken the trouble so much as to think out the nature of the true connection between wages and work, and to determine, even approximately, the real quantity of the one, that can, according to the laws of God and nature, be given for the other; for, rely on it, make what laws you like, that quantity only can you at last get.

10. "Do you know how many mouths can be fed on an acre of land, or how fast those mouths multiply? and have you considered what is to be done finally with unfeedable mouths? 'Send them to be fed elsewhere,' do you say? Have you, then, formed any opinion as to the time at which emigration should begin, or the countries to which it should preferably take place, or the kind of population which should be left at home? Have you planned the permanent state which you would wish England to hold, emigrating over her edges, like a full well, constantly? How full would you have her be of people, first? and of what sort of people? Do you want her to be nothing but a large workshop and forge, so that the name of 'Englishman' shall be synonymous with 'ironmonger,' all over the world? or would you like to keep some of your lords and landed gentry still, and a few green fields and trees?

11. "You know well enough that there is not one of these questions, I do not say which

you can answer, but which you have ever *thought* of answering; and yet you want to have voices in Parliament! Your voices are not worth a rat's squeak, either in Parliament or out of it, till you have some ideas to utter with them; and when you have the thoughts, you will not want to utter them, for you will see that your way to the fulfilling of them does not lie through speech. You think such matters need debating about? By all means debate about them; but debate among yourselves, and with such honest helpers of your thoughts as you can find; if by that way you cannot get at the truth, do you suppose you could get at it sooner in the House of Commons, where the only aim of many of the members would be to refute every word uttered in your favour; and where the settlement of any question whatever depends merely on the perturbations of the balance of conflicting interests?"

12. That was, in main particulars, what I then said to the men of the Working Men's College; and in this recurrent agitation about Reform, that is what I would steadfastly say again. Do you think it is only under the lacquered splendours of Westminster,—you working

men of England,—that your affairs can be rationally talked over? You have perfect liberty and power to talk over, and establish for yourselves, whatever laws you please; so long as you do not interfere with other people's liberties or properties. Elect a parliament of your own. Choose the best men among you, the best at least you can find, by whatever system of election you think likeliest to secure such desirable result. Invite trustworthy persons of other classes to join your council; appoint time and place for its stated sittings, and let this parliament, chosen after your own hearts, deliberate upon the possible modes of the regulation of industry, and advisablest schemes for helpful discipline of life; and so lay before you the best laws they can devise, which such of you as were wise might submit to, and teach their children to obey. And if any of the laws thus determined appear to be inconsistent with the present circumstances or customs of trade, do not make a noise about them, nor try to enforce them suddenly on others, nor embroider them on flags, nor call meetings in parks about them, in spite of railings and police; but keep them in your thoughts and sight, as objects of patient purpose and future achievement by peaceful strength.

13. For you need not think that even if you obtained a majority of representatives in the existing parliament, you could immediately compel any system of business, broadly contrary to that now established by custom. If you could pass laws to-morrow, wholly favourable to yourselves, as you might think, because unfavourable to your masters, and to the upper classes of society,—the only result would be that the riches of the country would at once leave it, and you would perish in riot and famine. Be assured that no great change for the better can ever be easily accomplished, or quickly; nor by impulsive, ill-regulated effort, nor by bad men ; nor even by good men, without much suffering. The suffering must, indeed, come, one way or another, in all greatly critical periods ; the only question, for us, is whether we will reach our ends (if we ever reach them) through a chain of involuntary miseries, many of them useless, and all ignoble ; or whether we will know the worst at once, and deal with it by the wisely sharp methods of Godsped courage.

14. This, I repeat to you, it is wholly in your own power to do, but it is in your power on one condition only, that of steadfast truth to yourselves, and to all men. If there is not, in the sum of it, honesty enough among you to teach you to frame, and strengthen you to obey, *just* laws of trade, there is no hope left for you. No political constitution can ennoble knaves; no privileges can assist them; no possessions enrich them. Their gains are occult curses; comfortless loss their truest blessing; failure and pain Nature's only mercy to them. Look to it, therefore, first, that you get some wholesome honesty for the foundation of all things. Without the resolution in your hearts to do good work, so long as your right hands have motion in them; and to do it whether the issue be that you die or live, no life worthy the name will ever be possible to you, while, in once forming the resolution that your work is to be well done, life is really won, here and for ever. And to make your children capable of such resolution, is the beginning of all true education, of which I have more to say in a future letter.

LETTER IV.

The Expenses for Art and for War.

February 19, 1867.

15. IN the 'Pall Mall Gazette' of yesterday, second column of second page, you will find, close to each other, two sentences which bear closely on matters in hand. The first of these is the statement, that in the debate on the grant for the Blacas collection, "Mr. Bernal Osborne got an assenting cheer, when he said that 'whenever science and art were mentioned it was a sign to look after the national pockets.'" I want you to notice this fact, *i.e.*, (the debate in question being on a *total* grant of 164,000*l.*, of which 48,000*l.* only were truly for art's sake, and the rest for shop's sake,) in illustration of a passage in my 'Sesame and Lilies' (pp. 69, 70 of the small edition, and pp. 46, 47 of Vol. I. of the Revised Series of the Entire Works),*

* Appendix I.

to which I shall have again to refer you, with some further comments, in the sequel of these letters. The second passage is to the effect that "'The Trades' Union Bill was read a second time, after a claim from Mr. Hadfield, Mr. Osborne, and Mr. Samuelson, to admit working men into the commission; to which Mr. Watkin answered 'that the working men's friend was too conspicuous in the body;' and Mr. Roebuck, 'that when a butcher was tried for murder it was not necessary to have butchers on the jury.'"

16. Note this second passage with respect to what I said in my last letter, as to the impossibility of the laws of work being investigated in the House of Commons. What admixture of elements, think you, would avail to obtain so much as decent hearing (how should we then speak of impartial judgment?) of the cause of working men, in an assembly which permits to one of its principal members this insolent discourtesy of language, in dealing with a preliminary question of the highest importance; and permits it as so far expressive of the whole colour and tone of its own thoughts, that the sentence is quoted by

one of the most temperate and accurate of our daily journals, as representing the total answer of the opposite side in the debate? No! be assured you can do nothing yet at Westminster. You must have your own parliament, and if you cannot detect enough honesty among you to constitute a justly minded one, for the present matters must take their course, and that will be, yet awhile, to the worse.

17. I meant to have continued this subject, but I see two other statements in the 'Pall Mall Gazette' of to-day, with which, and a single remark upon them, I think it will be well to close my present letter.

(1) "The total sum asked for in the army estimates, published this morning, is 14,752,200*l*., being an increase of 412,000*l*. over the previous year."

(2) "Yesterday the annual account of the navy receipts and expenditure for the year ending 31st March, 1866, was issued from the Admiralty. The expenditure was 10,268,115*l*. 7*s*."

Omitting the seven shillings, and even the odd hundred-thousands of pounds, the net annual expenditure for army and navy appears to be twenty-four millions.

The "grant in science and art," two-thirds of which was not in reality for either, but for amusement and shop interests in the Paris Exhibition—the grant which the House of Commons feels to be indicative of general danger to the national pockets—is, as above stated, 164,000*l.* Now, I believe the three additional ciphers which turn thousands into millions produce on the intelligent English mind usually the effect of—three ciphers. But calculate the proportion of these two sums, and then imagine to yourself the beautiful state of rationality of any private gentleman, who, having regretfully spent 164*l.* on pictures for his walls, paid willingly 24,000*l.* annually to the policeman who looked after his shutters! You practical English!—will you ever unbar the shutters of your brains, and hang a picture or two in *those* state-chambers?

LETTER V.

The Corruption of Modern Pleasure.—(Covent Garden Pantomime.)

February 25, 1867.

18. THERE is this great advantage in the writing real letters, that the direct correspondence is a sufficient reason for saying, in or out of order, everything that the chances of the day bring into one's head, in connection with the matter in hand; and as such things very usually go out of one's head again, after they get tired of their lodging, they would otherwise never get said at all. And thus to-day, quite out of order, but in very close connection with another part of our subject, I am going to tell you what I was thinking on Friday evening last, in Covent Garden Theatre, as I was looking, and not laughing, at the pantomime of 'Ali Baba and the Forty Thieves.'

When you begin seriously to consider the

question referred to in my second letter, of the essential, and in the outcome inviolable, connection between quantity of wages, and quantity of work, you will see that "wages" in the full sense don't mean "pay" merely, but the reward, whatever it may be, of pleasure as well as profit, and of various other advantages, which a man is meant by Providence to get during life, for work well done. Even limiting the idea to "pay," the question is not so much what quantity of coin you get, as—what you can get for it when you have it. Whether a shilling a day be good pay or not, depends wholly on what a "shilling's worth" is; that is to say, what quantity of the things you want may be had for a shilling. And that again depends, and a great deal more than that depends, on what you *do* want. If only drink, and foul clothes, such and such pay may be enough for you; if you want good meat and good clothes, you must have larger wage; if clean rooms and fresh air, larger still, and so on. You say, perhaps, "every one wants these better things." So far from that, a wholesome taste for cleanliness and fresh air is one of the final attainments of humanity. There are now not many European gentlemen, even in the highest classes, who have a pure and right love of fresh air. They would put the filth of tobacco even into the first breeze of a May morning.

19. But there are better things even than these, which one may want. Grant that one has good food, clothes, lodging, and breathing, is that all the pay one ought to have for one's work? Wholesome means of existence and nothing more? Enough, perhaps, you think, if everybody could get these. It may be so; I will not, at this moment, dispute it; nevertheless, I will boldly say that you should sometimes want more than these; and for one of many things more, you should want occasionally to be amused!

You know, the upper classes, most of them, want to be amused all day long. They think

> "One moment *un*amused a misery
> Not made for feeble men."

Perhaps you have been in the habit of despising them for this; and thinking how much worthier and nobler it was to work all day, and care at night only for food and rest, than to do no useful thing all day, eat unearned food, and spend the evening, as the morning, in "change of follies and relays of joy." No, my good friend, that is one of the fatallest deceptions. It is not a noble thing, in sum and issue of it, not to care to be amused. It is indeed a far higher *moral* state, but is a much lower *creature* state, than that of the upper classes.

20. Yonder poor horse, calm slave in daily chains at the railroad siding, who drags the detached rear of the train to the front again, and slips aside so deftly as the buffers meet; and, within eighteen inches of death every ten minutes, fulfils his changeless duty all day long, content, for eternal reward, with his night's rest, and his champed mouthful of hay;—anything more earnestly moral and beautiful one cannot image—I never see the creature without a kind of worship. And yonder musician, who used the greatest power which (in the art he knew) the Father of spirits ever yet breathed into the clay of this world;—who used it, I say, to follow and fit with perfect sound the words of the 'Zauberflöte' and of 'Don Giovanni'—foolishest and most monstrous of conceivable human words and subjects of thought—for the future "amusement" of his race !—No such

spectacle of unconscious (and in that unconsciousness all the more fearful) moral degradation of the highest faculty to the lowest purpose can be found in history. But Mozart is nevertheless a nobler creature than the horse at the siding; nor would it be the least nearer the purpose of his Maker that he, and all his frivolous audiences, should evade the degradation of the profitless piping, only by living, like horses, in daily physical labour for daily bread.

21. There are three things to which man is born*—labour, and sorrow, and joy. Each of these three things has its baseness and its nobleness. There is base labour, and noble labour. There is base sorrow, and noble sorrow. There is base joy, and noble joy. But you must not think to avoid the corruption of these things by doing without the things themselves. Nor can any life be right that has not all three. Labour without joy is base. Labour without sorrow is base. Sorrow without labour is base. Joy without labour is base.

22. I dare say you think I am a long time in coming to the pantomime; I am not ready

---

* I ask the reader's thoughtful attention to this paragraph, on which much of what else I have to say depends.

to come to it yet in due course, for we ought to go and see the Japanese jugglers first, in order to let me fully explain to you what I mean. But I can't write much more to-day; so I shall merely tell you what part of the play set me thinking of all this, and leave you to consider of it yourself, till I can send you another letter. The pantomime was, as I said, 'Ali Baba and the Forty Thieves.' The forty thieves were girls. The forty thieves had forty companions, who were girls. The forty thieves and their forty companions were in some way mixed up with about four hundred and forty fairies, who were girls. There was an Oxford and Cambridge boat-race, in which the Oxford and Cambridge men were girls. There was a transformation scene, with a forest, in which the flowers were girls, and a chandelier, in which the lamps were girls, and a great rainbow which was all of girls.

23. Mingled incongruously with these seraphic, and, as far as my boyish experience extends, novel, elements of pantomime, there were yet some of its old and fast-expiring elements. There were, in speciality, two thoroughly good pantomime actors—Mr. W. H. Payne and Mr.

Frederick Payne. All that these two did, was done admirably. There were two subordinate actors, who played, subordinately well, the fore and hind legs of a donkey. And there was a little actress of whom I have chiefly to speak, who played exquisitely the little part she had to play. The scene in which she appeared was the only one in the whole pantomime in which there was any dramatic effort, or, with a few rare exceptions, any dramatic possibility. It was the home scene, in which Ali Baba's wife, on washing day, is called upon by butcher, baker, and milkman, with unpaid bills; and in the extremity of her distress hears her husband's knock at the door, and opens it for him to drive in his donkey, laden with gold. The children who have been beaten instead of getting breakfast, presently share in the raptures of their father and mother; and the little lady I spoke of, eight or nine years old,—dances a *pas-de-deux* with the donkey.

24. She did it beautifully and simply, as a child ought to dance. She was not an infant prodigy; there was no evidence, in the finish or strength of her motion, that she had been put to continual torture through half her eight or

nine years. She did nothing more than any child, well taught, but painlessly, might easily do. She caricatured no older person,—attempted no curious or fantastic skill. She was dressed decently,—she moved decently,—she looked and behaved innocently,—and she danced her joyful dance with perfect grace, spirit, sweetness, and self-forgetfulness. And through all the vast theatre, full of English fathers and mothers and children, there was not one hand lifted to give her sign of praise but mine.

Presently after this, came on the forty thieves, who, as I told you, were girls; and, there being no thieving to be presently done, and time hanging heavy on their hands, arms, and legs, the forty thief-girls proceeded to light forty cigars. Whereupon the British public gave them a round of applause. Whereupon I fell a thinking; and saw little more of the piece, except as an ugly and disturbing dream.

LETTER VI.

The Corruption of Modern Pleasure.—(The Japanese Jugglers.)

February 28, 1867.

25. I HAVE your pleasant letter with references to Frederick. I will look at them carefully.* Mr. Carlyle himself will be pleased to hear this letter when he comes home. I heard from him last week at Mentone. He is well, and glad of the light and calm of Italy. I must get back to the evil light and uncalm, of the places I was taking you through.

(Parenthetically, did you see the article in the 'Times' of yesterday on bribery, and the conclusion of the commission—" No one sold any opinions, for no one had any opinions to sell "?)

Both on Thursday and Friday last I had been tormented by many things, and wanted to

* Appendix 2.

disturb my course of thought any way I could. I have told you what entertainment I got on Friday, first, for it was then that I began meditating over these letters; let me tell you now what entertainment I found on Thursday.

26. You may have heard that a company of Japanese jugglers has come over to exhibit in London. There has long been an increasing interest in Japanese art, which has been very harmful to many of our own painters, and I greatly desired to see what these people were, and what they did. Well, I have seen Blondin, and various English and French circus work, but never yet anything that surprised me so much as one of these men's exercises on a suspended pole. Its special character was a close approximation to the action and power of the monkey; even to the prehensile power in the foot; so that I asked a sculptor-friend who sat in front of me, whether he thought such a grasp could be acquired by practice, or indicated difference in race. He said he thought it might be got by practice. There was also much inconceivably dexterous work in spinning of tops,—making them pass in balanced motion along the edge of a sword, and along a level

VI. DEXTERITY. 35

string, and the like;—the father performing in the presence of his two children, who encouraged him continually with short, sharp cries, like those of animals. Then there was some fairly good sleight-of-hand juggling of little interest; ending with a dance by the juggler, first as an animal, and then as a goblin. Now, there was this great difference between the Japanese masks used in this dance and our common pantomime masks for beasts and demons,—that our English masks are only stupidly and loathsomely ugly, by exaggeration of feature, or of defect of feature. But the Japanese masks (like the frequent monsters of Japanese art) were inventively frightful, like fearful dreams; and whatever power it is that acts on human minds, enabling them to invent such, appears to me not only to deserve the term "demoniacal," as the only word expressive of its character; but to be logically capable of no other definition.

27. The impression, therefore, produced upon me by the whole scene, was that of being in the presence of human creatures of a partially inferior race, but not without great human gentleness, domestic affection, and ingenious intellect; who were, nevertheless, as a nation,

afflicted by an evil spirit, and driven by it to recreate themselves in achieving, or beholding the achievement, through years of patience, of a certain correspondence with the nature of the lower animals.

28. These, then, were the two forms of diversion or recreation of my mind possible to me, in two days, when I needed such help, in this metropolis of England. I might, as a rich man, have had better music, if I had so chosen, though, even so, not rational or helpful; but a poor man could only have these, or worse than these, if he cared for any manner of spectacle. (I am not at present, observe, speaking of pure acting, which is a study, and recreative only as a noble book is; but of means of *mere* amusement.)

Now, lastly, in illustration of the effect of these and other such "amusements," and of the desire to obtain them, on the minds of our youth, read the 'Times' correspondent's letter from Paris, in the tenth page of the paper, to-day;* and that will be quite enough for you to read, for the present, I believe.

* Appendix 3.

LETTER VII.

Of the various Expressions of National Festivity.

March 4, 1867.

29. THE subject which I want to bring before you is now branched, and worse than branched, reticulated, in so many directions, that I hardly know which shoot of it to trace, or which knot to lay hold of first.

I had intended to return to those Japanese jugglers, after a visit to a theatre in Paris; but I had better, perhaps, at once tell you the piece of the performance which, in connection with the scene in the English pantomime, bears most on matters in hand.

It was also a dance by a little girl—though one older than Ali Baba's daughter, (I suppose a girl of twelve or fourteen). A dance, so called, which consisted only in a series of short, sharp contractions and jerks of the body and limbs, resulting in attitudes of distorted and quaint ugliness, such as might be produced in a puppet by sharp twitching of strings at its joints: these movements being made to the sound of two instruments, which between them accomplished only a quick vibratory beating and strumming, in nearly the time of a hearth-cricket's song, but much harsher, and of course louder, and without any sweetness; only in the monotony and unintended aimless construction of it, reminding one of various other insect and reptile cries or warnings: partly of the cicala's hiss; partly of the little melancholy German frog which says "Mu, mu, mu," all summer-day long, with its nose out of the pools by Dresden and Leipsic; and partly of the deadened quivering and intense continuousness of the alarm of the rattlesnake.

While this was going on, there was a Bible text repeating itself over and over again in my head, whether I would or no:—"And Miriam the prophetess, the sister of Aaron, took a timbrel in her hand, and all the women went out after her with timbrels and with dances." To which text and some others, I shall ask your attention presently; but I must go to Paris first.

30. Not at once, however, to the theatre, but to a bookseller's shop, No. 4, Rue Voltaire,

where, in the year 1858, was published the fifth edition of Balzac's ' Contes Drôlatiques," illustrated by 425 designs by Gustave Doré.

Both text and illustrations are as powerful as it is ever in the nature of evil things to be—(there is no *final* strength but in rightness). Nothing more witty, nor more inventively horrible, has yet been produced in the evil literature, or by the evil art, of man : nor can I conceive it possible to go beyond either in their specialities of corruption. The text is full of blasphemies, subtle, tremendous, hideous in shamelessness, some put into the mouths of priests ; the illustrations are, in a word, one continuous revelry in the most loathsome and monstrous aspects of death and sin, enlarged into fantastic ghastliness of caricature, as if seen through the distortion and trembling of the hot smoke of the mouth of hell. Take this following for a general type of what they seek in death : one of the most laboured designs is of a man cut in two, downwards, by the sweep of a sword— one half of him falls towards the spectator ; the other half is elaborately drawn in its section—giving the profile of the divided nose and lips ; cleft jaw—breast—and entrails ; and this is done with farther pollution and horror of intent in the circumstances, which I do not choose to describe—still less some other of the designs which seek for fantastic extreme of sin, as this for the utmost horror of death. But of all the 425, there is not one, which does not violate every instinct of decency and law of virtue or life, written in the human soul.

31. Now, my friend, among the many "Signs of the Times" the production of a book like this is a significant one: but it becomes more significant still when connected with the farther fact, that M. Gustave Doré, the designer of this series of plates, has just been received with loud acclaim by the British Evangelical Public, as the fittest and most able person whom they could at present find to illustrate, to their minds, and recommend with grace of sacred art, their hitherto unadorned Bible for them.

Of which Bible, and of the use we at present make of it in England, having a grave word or two to say in my next letter (preparatory to the examination of that verse which haunted me through the Japanese juggling, and of some others also), I leave you first this sign of the public esteem of it to consider at your leisure.

LETTER VIII.

The Four possible Theories respecting the Authority of the Bible.

March 7, 1867.

32. I HAVE your yesterday's letter, but must not allow myself to be diverted from the business in hand for this once, for it is the most important of which I have to write to you.

You must have seen long ago that the essential difference between the political economy I am trying to teach, and the popular science, is, that mine is based on *presumably attainable honesty* in men, and conceivable respect in them for the interests of others, while the popular science founds itself wholly on their supposed constant regard for their own, and on their honesty only so far as thereby likely to be secured.

It becomes, therefore, for me, and for all who believe anything I say, a great primal question on what this presumably attainable honesty is to be based.

33. "Is it to be based on religion?" you may ask. "Are we to be honest for fear of losing heaven if we are dishonest, or (to put it as generously as we may) for fear of displeasing God? Or, are we to be honest on speculation, because honesty is the best policy; and to invest in virtue as in an undepreciable stock?"

And my answer is—not in any hesitating or diffident way (and you know, my friend, that whatever people may say of me, I often do speak diffidently; though, when I am diffident of things, I like to avoid speaking of them, if it may be; but here I say with no shadow of doubt)—your honesty is *not* to be based either on religion or policy. Both your religion and policy must be based on *it*. Your honesty must be based, as the sun is, in vacant heaven; poised, as the lights in the firmament, which have rule over the day and over the night. If you ask why you are to be honest—you are, in the question itself, dishonoured. "Because you are a man," is the only answer; and therefore I said in a former letter that to make your children *capable of honesty* is the beginning of education. Make them men first, and religious men afterwards, and all will be sound; but a knave's religion is always the rottenest thing about him.

34. It is not, therefore, because I am endeavouring to lay down a foundation of religious concrete, on which to build piers of policy, that you so often find me quoting Bible texts in defence of this or that principle or assertion. But the fact that such references are an offence, as I know them to be, to many of the readers of these political essays, is one among many others, which I would desire you to reflect upon (whether you are yourself one of the offended or not), as expressive of the singular position which the mind of the British public has at present taken with respect to its worshipped Book. The positions, honestly tenable, before I use any more of its texts, I must try to define for you.

35. All the theories possible to theological disputants respecting the Bible are resolvable into four, and four only.

(1.) The first is that of the illiterate modern religious world, that every word of the book known to them as "The Bible" was dictated by the Supreme Being, and is in every syllable of it His "Word."

This theory is of course tenable by no ordinarily well-educated person.

(2.) The second theory is, that, although admitting verbal error, the substance of the whole collection of books called the Bible is absolutely true, and furnished to man by Divine inspiration of the speakers and writers of it; and that every one who honestly and prayerfully seeks for such truth in it as is necessary for his salvation, will infallibly find it there.

This theory is that held by most of our good and upright clergymen, and the better class of the professedly religious laity.

(3.) The third theory is that the group of books which we call the Bible were neither written nor collected under any Divine guidance, securing them from substantial error; and that they contain, like all other human writings, false statements mixed with true, and erring thoughts mixed with just thoughts; but that they nevertheless relate, on the whole, faithfully, the dealings of the one God with the first races of man, and His dealings with them in aftertime through Christ: that they record true miracles, and bear true witness to the resurrection of the dead, and the life of the world to come.

This is a theory held by many of the active leaders of modern thought.

(4.) The fourth, and last possible, theory is that the mass of religious Scripture contains merely the best efforts which we hitherto know to have been made by any of the races of men towards the discovery of some relations with the spiritual world; that they are only trustworthy as expressions of the enthusiastic visions or beliefs of earnest men oppressed by the world's darkness, and have no more authoritative claim on our faith than the religious speculations and histories of the Egyptians, Greeks, Persians, and Indians; but are, in common with all these, to be reverently studied, as containing a portion, divinely appointed, of the best wisdom which human intellect, earnestly seeking for help from God, has hitherto been able to gather between birth and death.

This has been, for the last half-century, the theory of the soundest scholars and thinkers of Europe.

36. There is yet indeed one farther condition of incredulity attainable, and sorrowfully

attained, by many men of powerful intellect —the incredulity, namely, of inspiration in any sense, or of help given by any Divine power to the thoughts of men. But this form of infidelity merely indicates a natural incapacity for receiving certain emotions; though many honest and good men belong to this insentient class.

37. The educated men, therefore, who may be seriously appealed to, in these days, on questions of moral responsibility, as modified by Scripture, are broadly divisible into three classes, severally holding the last three theories above stated.

Now, whatever power a passage from the statedly authoritative portions of the Bible may have over the mind of a person holding the fourth theory, it will have a proportionately greater over that of persons holding the third or the second. I, therefore, always imagine myself speaking to the fourth class of theorists. If I can persuade or influence *them*, I am logically sure of the others. I say "logically," for the actual fact, strange as it may seem, is that no persons are so little likely to submit to a passage of Scripture not to their fancy, as those who are most positive on the subject of its general inspiration.

38. Addressing, then, this fourth class of thinkers, I would say to them, when asking them to enter on any subject of importance to national morals, or conduct, "This book, which has been the accepted guide of the moral intelligence of Europe for some fifteen hundred years, enforces certain simple laws of human conduct which you know have also been agreed upon, in every main point, by all the religious, and by all the greatest profane writers, of every age and country. This book primarily forbids pride, lasciviousness, and covetousness; and you know that all great thinkers, in every nation of mankind, have similarly forbidden these mortal vices. This book enjoins truth, temperance, charity, and equity; and you know that every great Egyptian, Greek, and Indian, enjoins these also. You know besides, that through all the mysteries of human fate and history, this one great law of fate is written on the walls of cities, or in their dust; written in letters of light, and letters of blood,—that where truth, temperance, and equity have been preserved, all strength, and peace, and joy have been preserved also;—that where lying, lasciviousness, and covetousness have been practised, there has

followed an infallible, and, for centuries, irrecoverable ruin. And you know, lastly, that the observance of this common law of righteousness, commending itself to all the pure instincts of men, and fruitful in their temporal good, is by the religious writers of every nation, and chiefly in this venerated Scripture of ours, connected with some distinct hope of better life, and righteousness, to come.

39. "Let it not then offend you if, deducing principles of action first from the laws and facts of nature, I nevertheless fortify them also by appliance of the precepts, or suggestive and probable teachings of this Book, of which the authority is over many around you, more distinctly than over you, and which, confessing to be divine, *they*, at least, can only disobey at their moral peril."

On these grounds, and in this temper, I am in the habit of appealing to passages of Scripture in my writings on political economy; and in this temper I will ask you to consider with me some conclusions which appear to me derivable from that text about Miriam, which haunted me through the jugglery; and from certain others.

LETTER IX.

The Use of Music and Dancing under the Jewish Theocracy, compared with their Use by the Modern French.

March 10, 1867.

40. HAVING, I hope, made you now clearly understand with what feeling I would use the authority of the book which the British public, professing to consider sacred, have lately adorned for themselves with the work of the boldest violator of the instincts of human honour and decency known yet in art-history, I will pursue by the help of that verse about Miriam, and some others, the subject which occupied my mind at both theatres, and to which, though in so apparently desultory manner, I have been nevertheless very earnestly endeavouring to lead you.

41. The going forth of the women of Israel after Miriam with timbrels and with dances, was, as you doubtless remember, their expression of passionate triumph and thankfulness,

after the full accomplishment of their deliverance from the Egyptians. That deliverance had been by the utter death of their enemies, and accompanied by stupendous miracle; no human creatures could in an hour of triumph be surrounded by circumstances more solemn. I am not going to try to excite your feelings about them. Consider only for yourself what that seeing of the Egyptians "dead upon the sea-shore" meant to every soul that saw it. And then reflect that these intense emotions of mingled horror, triumph, and gratitude were expressed, in the visible presence of the Deity, by music and dancing. If you answer that you do not believe the Egyptians so perished, or that God ever appeared in a pillar of cloud, I reply, "Be it so—believe or disbelieve, as you choose;—This is yet assuredly the fact, that the author of the poem or fable of the Exodus supposed that, under such circumstances of Divine interposition as he had invented, the triumph of the Israelitish women would have been, and ought to have been, under the direction of a prophetess, expressed by music and dancing."

42. Nor was it possible that he should think otherwise, at whatever period he wrote;

both music and dancing being, among all great ancient nations, an appointed and very principal part of the worship of the gods.

And that very theatrical entertainment at which I sate thinking over these things for you —that pantomime, which depended throughout for its success on an appeal to the vices of the lower London populace, was, in itself, nothing but a corrupt remnant of the religious ceremonies which guided the most serious faiths of the Greek mind, and laid the foundation of their gravest moral and didactic—more forcibly so because at the same time dramatic— literature.

43. Returning to the Jewish history, you find soon afterwards this enthusiastic religious dance and song employed, in their more common and habitual manner, in the idolatries under Sinai; but beautifully again and tenderly, after the triumph of Jephthah, "And behold his daughter came out to meet him with timbrels and with dances." Again, still more notably, at the triumph of David with Saul, " the women came out of all the cities of Israel singing and dancing to meet King Saul with tabrets, with joy, and with instruments of music." And you

have this joyful song and dance of the virgins of Israel not only incidentally alluded to in the most solemn passages of Hebrew religious poetry (as in Psalm lxviii. 24, 25, and Psalm cxlix. 2, 3), but approved, and the restoration of it promised as a sign of God's perfect blessing, most earnestly by the saddest of the Hebrew prophets, and in one of the most beautiful of all his sayings.

"The Lord hath appeared of old unto me, saying, 'Yea, I have loved thee with an everlasting love. Therefore, with loving-kindness have I drawn thee.—I will build thee, and thou shalt be built, O Virgin of Israel; thou shalt again be adorned with thy tabrets, and thou shalt go forth in dances with them that make merry,'" (Jer. xxxi. 3, 4 ; and compare v. 13). And finally, you have in two of quite the most important passages in the whole series of Scripture (one in the Old Testament, one in the New), the rejoicing in the repentance from, and remission of, sins, expressed by means of music and dancing, namely, in the rapturous dancing of David before the returning ark ; and in the joy of the father's household at the repentance of the prodigal son.

44. I could put all this much better, and more convincingly, before you, if I were able to take any pains in writing at present; but I am not, as I told you; being weary and ill; neither do I much care now to use what, in the very truth, are but tricks of literary art, in dealing with this so grave subject. You see I write you my letter straightforward, and let you see all my scratchings out and puttings in; and if the way I say things shocks you, or any other reader of these letters, I cannot help it; this only I know, that what I tell you is true, and written more earnestly than anything I ever wrote with my best literary care; and that you will find it useful to think upon, however it be said. Now, therefore, to draw towards our conclusion. Supposing the Bible inspired, in any of the senses above defined, you have in these passages a positively Divine authority for the use of song and dance, as a means of religious service, and expression of national thanksgiving. Supposing it not inspired, you have (taking the passages for as slightly authoritative as you choose) record in them, nevertheless, of a state of mind in a great nation, producing the most beautiful religious poetry and perfect moral law hitherto

known to us, yet only expressible by them, to the fulfilment of their joyful passion, by means of professional dance and choral song.

45. Now I want you to contrast this state of religious rapture with some of our modern phases of mind in parallel circumstances. You see that the promise of Jeremiah's, " Thou shalt go forth in the dances of them that make merry," is immediately followed by this, " Thou shalt yet *plant vines* upon the mountains of Samaria." And again, at the yearly feast to the Lord in Shiloh, the dancing of the virgins was in the midst of the vineyards (Judges xxi. 21), the feast of the vintage being in the south, as our harvest home in the north, a peculiar occasion of joy and thanksgiving. I happened to pass the autumn of 1863 in one of the great vine districts of Switzerland, under the slopes of the outlying branch of the Jura which limits the arable plain of the Canton Zurich, some fifteen miles north of Zurich itself. That city has always been a renowned stronghold of Swiss Protestantism, next in importance only to Geneva; and its evangelical zeal for the conversion of the Catholics of Uri, and endeavours to bring about that spiritual result by stopping the

supplies of salt they needed to make their cheeses with, brought on (the Uri men reading their Matt. v. 13, in a different sense) the battle of Keppel, and the death of the reformer Zwinglius. The town itself shows the most gratifying signs of progress in all the modern arts and sciences of life. It is nearly as black as Newcastle—has a railroad station larger than the London terminus of the Chatham and Dover —fouls the stream of the Limmat as soon as it issues from the lake, so that you might even venture to compare the formerly simple and innocent Swiss river (I remember it thirty years ago—a current of pale green crystal) with the highly educated English streams of Weare or Tyne; and, finally, has as many French prints of dissolute tendency in its principal shop windows as if they had the privilege of opening on the Parisian Boulevards.

46. I was somewhat anxious to see what species of thanksgiving or exultation would be expressed at *their* vintage, by the peasantry in the neighbourhood of this much enlightened, evangelical, and commercial society. It consisted in two ceremonies only. During the day, the servants of the farms where the grapes

had been gathered, collected in knots about the vineyards, and slowly fired horse-pistols, from morning to evening. At night they got drunk, and staggered up and down the hill paths, uttering, at short intervals, yells and shrieks, differing only from the howling of wild animals by a certain intended and insolent discordance, only attainable by the malignity of debased human creatures.

47. I must not do the injustice to the Zurich peasantry of implying that this manner of festivity is peculiar to them. A year before, in 1862, I had formed the intention of living some years in the neighbourhood of Geneva, and had established myself experimentally on the eastern slope of the Mont Salève; but I was forced to abandon my purpose at last, because I could not endure the rabid howling, on Sunday evenings, of the holiday-makers who came out from Geneva to get drunk in the mountain village. By the way, your last letter, with its extracts about our traffic in gin, is very valuable. I will come to that part of the business in a little while. Meantime, my friend, note this, respecting what I have told you, that in the very centre of Europe, in a country which is visited for their

chief pleasure by the most refined and thoughtful persons among all Christian nations—a country made by God's hand the most beautiful in the temperate regions of the earth, and inhabited by a race once capable of the sternest patriotism and simplest purity of life, your modern religion, in the very stronghold of it, has reduced the song and dance of ancient virginal thanksgiving to the howlings and staggerings of men betraying, in intoxication, a nature sunk more than half-way towards the beasts; and you will begin to understand why the Bible should have been "illustrated" by Gustave Doré.

48. One word more is needful, though this letter is long already. The peculiar ghastliness of this Swiss mode of festivity is in its utter failure of joy; the paralysis and helplessness of a vice in which there is neither pleasure, nor art. But we are not, throughout Europe, wholly thus. There is such a thing, yet, as rapturous song and dance among us, though not indicative, by any means, of joy over repentant sinners. You must come back to Paris with me again. I had an evening to spare there, last summer, for investigation of

theatres; and as there was nothing at any of them that I cared much about seeing, I asked a valet-de-place at Meurice's what people were generally going to. He said, " All the English went to see the *Lanterne Magique.*" I do not care to tell you what general entertainment I received in following, for once, the lead of my countrymen; but it closed with the representation of the characteristic dancing of all ages of the world; and the dance given as characteristic of modern time was the Cancan, which you will see alluded to in the extract given in the note at page 80 of 'Sesame and Lilies' (the small edition; and page 54 of Vol. I. of the Revised Series of the Entire Works). "The ball terminated with a Devilish Chain and a Cancan of Hell, at seven in the morning." It was led by four principal dancers (who have since appeared in London in the *Huguenot Captain*), and it is many years since I have seen such perfect dancing, as far as finish and accuracy of art and fulness of animal power and fire are concerned. Nothing could be better done, in its own evil way, the object of the dance throughout being to express, in every gesture, the wildest fury of insolence and vicious passions possible to human creatures. So that you see, though, for the present, we find ourselves utterly incapable of a rapture of gladness or thanksgiving, the dance which is presented as characteristic of modern civilization is still rapturous enough—but it is with rapture of blasphemy.

LETTER X.

The Meaning and Actual Operation of Satanic or Demoniacal Influence.

March 16, 1867.

49. YOU may gather from the facts given you in my last letter that, as the expression of true and holy gladness was in old time statedly offered up by men for a part of worship to God their Father, so the expression of false and unholy gladness is in modern times, with as much distinctness and plainness, asserted by them openly to be offered to another spirit: "Chain of the Devil," and "Cancan of Hell" being the names assigned to these modern forms of joyous procession.

Now, you know that, among the best and wisest of our present religious teachers, there is a gradual tendency to disbelieve, and to preach their disbelief, in the commonly received ideas of the Devil, and of his place, and his work. While, among some of our equally well-meaning, but far less wise, religious teachers, there is, in consequence, a panic spreading in anticipation of the moral dangers which must follow on the loss of the help of the Devil. One of the last appearances in public of the author of the 'Christian Year' was at a conclave of clergymen assembled in defence of faith in damnation.* The sense of the meeting generally was, that there *must* be such a place as hell, because no one would ever behave decently upon earth unless they were kept in wholesome fear of the fires beneath it: and Mr. Keble, especially insisting on this view, related a story of an old woman who had a wicked son, and who, having lately heard with horror of the teaching of Mr. Maurice and others, exclaimed pathetically, "My son is bad enough as it is, and if he were not afraid of hell, what would become of him!" (I write from memory, and cannot answer for the words, but I can for their purport.)

50. Now, my friend, I am afraid that I must incur the charge of such presumption as may be involved in variance from *both* these systems of teaching.

* *Physical* damnation, I should have said. It is strange how seldom pain of heart is spoken of as a possible element of future, or as the worst of present pain.

I do not merely *believe* there is such a place as hell. I *know* there is such a place; and I know also that when men have got to the point of believing virtue impossible but through dread of it, they have got *into* it.

I mean, that according to the distinctness with which they hold such a creed, the stain of nether fire has passed upon them. In the depth of his heart Mr. Keble could not have entertained the thought for an instant; and I believe it was only as a conspicuous sign to the religious world of the state into which they were sinking, that this creed, possible in its sincerity only to the basest of them, was nevertheless appointed to be uttered by the lips of the most tender, gracious, and beloved of their teachers.

51. "Virtue impossible but for fear of hell"—a lofty creed for your English youth—and a holy one! And yet, my friend, there was something of right in the terrors of this clerical conclave. For, though you should assuredly be able to hold your own in the straight ways of God, without always believing that the Devil is at your side, it is a state of mind much to be dreaded, that you should not *know* the Devil when you *see* him there. For the probability is

that when you do see him, the way you are walking in is not one of God's ways at all, but is leading you quite into other neighbourhoods than His. On His way, indeed, you may often, like Albert Dürer's Knight, see the Fiend behind you, but you will find that he drops always farther and farther behind; whereas, if he jogs with you at your side, it is probably one of his own by-paths you are got on. And, in any case, it is a highly desirable matter that you should know him when you set eyes on him, which we are very far from doing in these days, having convinced ourselves that the graminivorous form of him, with horn and tail, is extant no longer. But in fearful truth, the Presence and Power of Him *is* here; in the world, with us, and within us, mock as you may; and the fight with him, for the time, sore, and widely unprosperous.

Do not think I am speaking metaphorically or rhetorically, or with any other than literal and earnest meaning of words. Hear me, I pray you, therefore, for a little while, as earnestly as I speak.

52. Every faculty of man's soul, and every instinct of it by which he is meant to live, is exposed to its own special form of corruption:

and whether within Man, or in the external world, there is a power or condition of temptation which is perpetually endeavouring to reduce every glory of his soul, and every power of his life, to such corruption as is possible to them. And the more beautiful they are, the more fearful is the death which is attached as a penalty to their degradation.

53. Take, for instance, that which, in its purity, is the source of the highest and purest mortal happiness—Love. Think of it first at its highest—as it may exist in the disciplined spirit of a perfect human creature; as it has so existed again and again, and does always, wherever it truly exists at all, as the *purifying* passion of the soul. I will not speak of the transcendental and imaginative intensity in which it may reign in noble hearts, as when it inspired the greatest religious poem yet given to men; but take it in its true and quiet purity in any simple lover's heart,—as you have it expressed, for instance, thus, exquisitely, in the 'Angel in the House':—

> "And there, with many a blissful tear,
> I vowed to love and prayed to wed
> The maiden who had grown so dear;—

X. WHEAT-SIFTING.

> Thanked God, who had set her in my path;
> And promised, as I hoped to win,
> I never would sully my faith
> By the least selfishness or sin;
> Whatever in her sight I'd seem
> I'd really be; I ne'er would blend,
> With my delight in her, a dream
> 'Twould change her cheek to comprehend;
> And, if she wished it, would prefer
> Another's to my own success;
> And always seek the best for her
> With unofficious tenderness."

Take this for the pure type of it in its simplicity; and then think of what corruption this passion is capable. I will give you a type of that also, and at your very doors. I cannot refer you to the time when the crime happened; but it was some four or five years ago, near Newcastle, and it has remained always as a ghastly landmark in my mind, owing to the horror of the external circumstances. The body of the murdered woman was found naked, rolled into a heap of ashes, at the mouth of one of your pits.

54. You have thus two limiting examples, of the Pure Passion, and of its corruption. Now, whatever influence it is, without or within us, which has a tendency to degrade the one

towards the other, is literally and accurately "Satanic." And this treacherous or deceiving spirit is perpetually at work, so that all the worst evil among us is a betrayed or corrupted good. Take religion itself: the desire of finding out God, and placing one's self in some true son's or servant's relation to Him. The Devil, that is to say, the deceiving spirit within us, or outside of us, mixes up our own vanity with this desire; makes us think that in our love to God we have established some connection with Him which separates us from our fellow-men, and renders us superior to them. Then it takes but one wave of the Devil's hand; and we are burning them alive for taking the liberty of contradicting us.

55. Take the desire of teaching—the entirely unselfish and noble instinct for telling to those who are ignorant, the truth we know, and guarding them from the errors we see them in danger of;—there is no nobler, no more constant instinct in honourable breasts; but let the Devil formalise it, and mix the pride of a profession with it—get foolish people entrusted with the business of instruction, and make their giddy heads giddier by putting them up in

pulpits above a submissive crowd—and you have it instantly corrupted into its own reverse; you have an alliance *against* the light, shrieking at the sun, and the moon, and stars, as profane spectra :—a company of the blind, beseeching those they lead to remain blind also. "The heavens and the lights that rule them are untrue; the laws of creation are treacherous; the poles of the earth are out of poise. But *we* are true. Light is in us only. Shut your eyes close and fast, and we will lead you."

56. Take the desire and faith of mutual help; the virtue of vowed brotherhood for the accomplishment of common purpose, (without which nothing great can be wrought by multitudinous bands of men); let the Devil put pride of caste into it, and you have a military organization applied for a thousand years to maintain that higher caste in idleness by robbing the labouring poor; let the Devil put a few small personal interests into it, and you have all faithful deliberation on national law rendered impossible in the parliaments of Europe, by the antagonism of parties.

57. Take the instinct for justice, and the natural sense of indignation against crime; let

the Devil colour it with personal passion, and you have a mighty race of true and tender-hearted men living for centuries in such bloody feud that every note and word of their national songs is a dirge, and every rock of their hills is a gravestone. Take the love of beauty, and power of imagination, which are the source of every true achievement in art; let the Devil touch them with sensuality, and they are stronger than the sword or the flame to blast the cities where they were born, into ruin without hope. Take the instinct of industry and ardour of commerce, which are meant to be the support and mutual maintenance of man; let the Devil touch them with avarice, and you shall see the avenues of the exchange choked with corpses that have died of famine.

58. Now observe—I leave you to call this deceiving spirit what you like—or to theorise about it as you like. All that I desire you to recognise is the fact of its being here, and the need of its being fought with. If you take the Bible's account of it, or Dante's, or Milton's, you will receive the image of it as a mighty spiritual creature, commanding others, and resisted by others: if you take Æschylus's or

Hesiod's account of it, you will hold it for a partly elementary and unconscious adversity of fate, and partly for a group of monstrous spiritual agencies connected with death, and begotten out of the dust; if you take a modern rationalist's, you will accept it for a mere treachery and want of vitality in our own moral nature exposing it to loathsomeness or moral disease, as the body is capable of mortification or leprosy. I do not care what you call it,—whose history you believe of it,—nor what you yourself can imagine about it; the origin, or nature, or name may be as you will, but the deadly reality of the thing is with us, and warring against us, and on our true war with it depends whatever life we can win. Deadly reality, I say. The puff-adder or horned asp is not more real. Unbelievable,—*those*,—unless you had seen them; no fable could have been coined out of any human brain so dreadful, within its own poor material sphere, as that blue-lipped serpent—working its way sidelong in the sand. As real, but with sting of eternal death —this worm that dies not, and fire that is not quenched, within our souls or around them. Eternal death, I say—sure, that, whatever creed you hold;—if the old Scriptural one, Death of perpetual banishment from before God's face; if the modern rationalist one, Death Eternal for *us*, instant and unredeemable ending of lives wasted in misery.

This is what this unquestionably present —this, according to his power, *omni*-present— fiend, brings us towards, daily. *He* is the person to be " voted " against, my working friend; it is worth something, having a vote against *him*, if you can get it! Which you can, indeed; but not by gift from Cabinet Ministers; you must work warily with your own hands, and drop sweat of heart's blood, before you can record that vote effectually.

Of which more in next letter.

LETTER XI.

The Satanic Power is mainly Twofold: the Power of causing Falsehood and the Power of causing Pain. The Resistance is by Law of Honour and Law of Delight.

March 19, 1857.

59. YOU may perhaps have thought my last three or four letters mere rhapsodies. They are nothing of the kind; they are accurate accounts of literal facts, which we have to deal with daily. This thing, or power, opposed to God's power, and specifically called "Mammon" in the Sermon on the Mount, is, in deed and in truth, a continually present and active enemy, properly called "*Arch*-enemy," that is to say, "Beginning and Prince of Enemies," and daily we have to record our vote for, or against him. Of the manner of which record we were next to consider.

60. This enemy is always recognisable, briefly in two functions. He is pre-eminently the Lord of *Lies* and the Lord of *Pain*.

Wherever Lies are, he is; wherever Pain is, he has been—so that of the Spirit of Wisdom (who is called God's Helper, as Satan His Adversary) it is written, not only that by her Kings reign, and Princes decree justice, but also that her ways are ways of Pleasantness, and all her paths Peace.

Therefore, you will succeed, you working men, in recording your votes against this arch-enemy, precisely in the degree in which you can do away with falsehood and pain in your work and lives; and bring truth into the one, and pleasure into the other; all education being directed to make yourselves and your children *capable of Honesty* and *capable of Delight;* and to rescue yourselves from iniquity and agony. And this is what I meant by saying in the preface to 'Unto this Last' that the central requirement of education consisted in giving habits of gentleness and justice; "gentleness" (as I will show you presently) being the best single word I could have used to express the capacity for giving and receiving true pleasure; and "justice" being similarly the most comprehensive word for all kind of honest dealing.

61. Now, I began these letters with the

purpose of explaining the nature of the requirements of justice first, and then those of gentleness, but I allowed myself to be led into that talk about the theatres, not only because the thoughts could be more easily written as they came, but also because I was able thus to illustrate for you more directly the nature of the enemy we have to deal with. You do not perhaps know, though I say this diffidently (for I often find working men know many things which one would have thought were out of their way), that music was, among the Greeks, quite the first means of education; and that it was so connected with their system of ethics and of intellectual training, that the God of Music is with them also the God of Righteousness;—the God who purges and avenges iniquity, and contends with their Satan as represented under the form of Python, "the corrupter." And the Greeks were incontrovertibly right in this. Music is the nearest at hand, the most orderly, the most delicate, and the most perfect, of all bodily pleasures; it is also the only one which is equally helpful to all the ages of man,—helpful from the nurse's song to her infant, to the music, unheard of others, which so often haunts the deathbed of pure and innocent spirits. And the action of the deceiving or devilish power is in *nothing* shown quite so distinctly among us at this day,—not even in our commercial dishonesties, nor in our social cruelties,—as in its having been able to take away music, as an instrument of education, altogether; and to enlist it almost wholly in the service of superstition on the one hand, and of sensuality on the other.

62. This power of the Muses, then, and its proper influence over you workmen, I shall eventually have much to insist upon with you; and in doing so I shall take that beautiful parable of the Prodigal Son (which I have already referred to), and explain, as far as I know, the significance of it, and then I will take the three means of festivity, or wholesome human joy, therein stated,—fine dress, rich food, and music;—("bring forth the fairest robe for him,"—"bring forth the fatted calf, and kill it;" "as he drew nigh, he heard music and dancing"); and I will show you how all these three things, fine dress, rich food, and music (including ultimately all the other arts)

are meant to be sources of life, and means of moral discipline, to all men; and how they have all three been made, by the Devil, the means of guilt, dissoluteness, and death.* But first I must return to my original plan of these letters, and endeavour to set down for you some of the laws which, in a true Working Men's Parliament, must be ordained in defence of Honesty.

Of which laws (preliminary to all others, and necessary above all others), having now somewhat got my ravelled threads together again, I will begin talk in my next letter.

* See 'Fors Clavigera,' Letter XXIV.

LETTER XII.

The Necessity of Imperative Law to the Prosperity of States.

March 20, 1867.

63. I HAVE your most interesting letter,* which I keep for reference, when I come to the consideration of its subject in its proper place, under the head of the abuse of Food. I do not wonder that your life should be rendered unhappy by the scenes of drunkenness which you are so often compelled to witness; nor that this so gigantic and infectious evil should seem to you the root of the greater part of the misery of our lower orders. I do not wonder that George Cruikshank has warped the entire current of his thoughts and life, at once to my admiration and my sorrow, from their natural field of work, that he might spend them, in struggle with this fiend, for the poor lowest people whom he knows so well.

* Appendix 4.

I wholly sympathise with you in indignation at the methods of temptation employed, and at the use of the fortunes made by the vendors of death; and whatever immediately applicable legal means there might be of restricting the causes of drunkenness, I should without hesitation desire to bring into operation. But all such appliance I consider temporary and provisionary; nor, while there is record of the miracle at Cana (not to speak of the sacrament) can I conceive it possible, without (logically) the denial of the entire truth of the New Testament, to reprobate the use of wine as a stimulus to the powers of life. Supposing we did deny the words and deeds of the Founder of Christianity, the authority of the wisest heathens, especially that of Plato in the 'Laws,' is wholly against abstinence from wine; and much as I can believe, and as I have been endeavouring to make you believe also, of the subtlety of the Devil, I do not suppose the vine to have been one of his inventions. Of this, however, more in another place. By the way, was it not curious that in the 'Manchester Examiner,' in which that letter of mine on the abuse of dancing appeared, there chanced to be, in the next column, a paragraph giving an account of a girl stabbing her betrayer in a ball-room; and another paragraph describing a Parisian character, which gives exactly the extreme type I wanted, for example of the abuse of Food?*

64. I return, however, now to the examination of possible means for the enforcement of justice, in temper and in act, as the first of political requirements. And as, in stating my conviction of the necessity of certain stringent laws on this matter, I shall be in direct opposition to Mr. Stuart Mill; and, more or less, in opposition to other professors of modern political economy, as well as to many honest and active promoters of the privileges of working men (as if privilege only were wanted and never restraint!), I will give you, as briefly as I can, the grounds on which I am prepared to justify such opposition.

65. When the crew of a wrecked ship escape in an open boat, and the boat is crowded, the provisions scanty, and the prospect of making land distant, laws are instantly established and enforced which no one thinks of disobeying. An entire equality of claim to the provisions is

* Appendix 5.

acknowledged without dispute; and an equal liability to necessary labour. No man who can row is allowed to refuse his oar; no man, however much money he may have saved in his pocket, is allowed so much as half a biscuit beyond his proper ration. Any riotous person who endangered the safety of the rest would be bound, and laid in the bottom of the boat, without the smallest compunction, for such violation of the principles of individual liberty; and, on the other hand, any child, or woman, or aged person, who was helpless, and exposed to great danger and suffering by their weakness, would receive more than ordinary care and indulgence, not unaccompanied with unanimous self-sacrifice on the part of the labouring crew.

There is never any question under circumstances like these, of what is right and wrong, worthy and unworthy, wise or foolish. If there *be* any question, there is little hope for boat or crew. The right man is put at the helm; every available hand is set to the oars; the sick are tended, and the vicious restrained, at once, and decisively; or if not, the end is near.

66. Now, the circumstances of every associated group of human society, contending

bravely for national honours and felicity of life, differ only from those thus supposed, in the greater, instead of less, necessity for the establishment of restraining law. There is no point of difference in the difficulties to be met, nor in the rights reciprocally to be exercised. Vice and indolence are not less, but more, injurious in a nation than in a boat's company; the modes in which they affect the interests of worthy persons being far more complex, and more easily concealed. The right of restraint, vested in those who labour, over those who would impede their labour, is as absolute in the large as in the small society; the equal claim to share in whatever is necessary to the common life (or commonwealth) is as indefeasible; the claim of the sick and helpless to be cared for by the strong with earnest self-sacrifice, is as pitiful and as imperative; the necessity that the governing authority should be in the hands of a true and trained pilot is as clear and as constant. In none of these conditions is there any difference between a nation and a boat's company. The only difference is in this, that the impossibility of discerning the effects of individual error and crime, or of counteracting them by individual effort, in the affairs of a great nation renders it tenfold more necessary than in a small society that direction by law should be sternly established. Assume that your boat's crew is disorderly and licentious, and will, by agreement, submit to no order;—the most troublesome of them will yet be easily discerned; and the chance is that the best man among them knocks him down. Common instinct of self-preservation will make the rioters put a good sailor at the helm, and impulsive pity and occasional help will be, by heart and hand, here and there given to visible distress. Not so in the ship of the realm. The most troublesome persons in *it* are usually the least recognised for such, and the most active in its management; the best men mind their own business patiently, and are never thought of; the good helmsman never touches the tiller but in the last extremity; and the worst forms of misery are hidden, not only from every eye, but from every thought. On the deck, the aspect is of Cleopatra's galley—under hatches there is a slave hospital; while, finally (and this is the most fatal difference of all), even the few persons who care to interfere energetically, with purpose of doing good, can, in a large society, discern so little of the real state of evil to be dealt with, and judge so little of the best means of dealing with it, that half of their best efforts will be misdirected, and some may even do more harm than good. Whereas it is the sorrowful law of this universe, that evil, even unconscious and unintended, never fails of *its* effect; and in a state where the evil and the good, under conditions of individual "liberty," are allowed to contend together, not only every *stroke* on the Devil's side tells—but every *slip*, (the mistakes of wicked men being as mischievous as their successes); while on the side of right, there will be much direct and fatal defeat, and, even of its measure of victory, half will be fruitless.

67. It is true, of course, that, in the end of ends, nothing but the right conquers; the prevalent thorns of wrong, at last, crackle away in indiscriminate flame: and of the good seed sown, one grain in a thousand some day comes up—and somebody lives by it; but most of our great teachers, not excepting Carlyle and Emerson themselves, are a little too encouraging in their proclamation of this comfort, not, to my

mind, very sufficient, when for the present our fields are full of nothing but darnel instead of wheat, and cockle instead of barley; and none of them seem to me yet to have enough insisted on the inevitable power and infectiousness of all evil, and the easy and utter extinguishableness of good. <u>Medicine often fails of its effect—but poison never</u>: and while, in summing the observation of past life, not unwatchfully spent, I can truly say that I have a thousand times seen patience disappointed of her hope, and wisdom of her aim, I have never yet seen folly fruitless of mischief, nor vice conclude but in calamity.

68. There, is, however, one important condition in national economy, in which the analogy of that of a ship's company is incomplete: namely, that while labour at oar or sail is necessarily united, and can attain no independent good, or personal profit, the labour properly undertaken by the several members of a political community is necessarily, and justly, within certain limits, independent; and obtains for them independent advantage, of which, if you will glance at the last paragraph of the first chapter of 'Munera Pulveris,' you will see I

should be the last person to propose depriving them. This great difference in final condition involves necessarily much complexity in the system and application of general laws; but it in no wise abrogates,—on the contrary, it renders yet more imperative,—the necessity for the firm ordinance of such laws, which, marking the due limits of independent agency, may enable it to exist in full energy, not only without becoming injurious, but so as more variously and perfectly to promote the entire interests of the commonwealth.

I will address myself therefore in my next letter to the statement of some of these necessary laws.

LETTER XIII.

The Proper Offices of the Bishop and Duke; or, "Overseer" and "Leader."

March 21, 1867.

69. I SEE, by your last letter, for which I heartily thank you, that you would not sympathise with me in my sorrow for the desertion of his own work by George Cruikshank, that he may fight in the front of the temperance ranks. But you do not know what work he has left undone, nor how much richer inheritance you might have received from his hand. It was no more *his* business to etch diagrams of drunkenness than it is mine at this moment to be writing these letters against anarchy. It is "the first mild day of March" (high time, I think, that it should be!), and by rights I ought to be out among the budding banks and hedges, outlining sprays of hawthorn and clusters of primrose. That is *my* right work; and it is not, in the inner gist and truth of it, right nor good, for you, or for anybody else, that Cruikshank with his great gift, and I with my weak,

but yet thoroughly clear and definite one, should both of us be tormented by agony of indignation and compassion, till we are forced to give up our peace, and pleasure, and power; and rush down into the streets and lanes of the city, to do the little that is in the strength of our single hands against their uncleanliness and iniquity. But, as in a sorely besieged town, every man must to the ramparts, whatsoever business he leaves, so neither he nor I have had any choice but to leave our household stuff, and go on crusade, such as we are called to; not that I mean, if Fate may be anywise resisted, to give up the strength of my life, as he has given his; for I think he was wrong in doing so; and that he should only have carried the fiery cross his appointed leagues, and then given it to another hand; and, for my own part, I mean these very letters to close my political work for many a day; and I write them, not in any hope of their being at present listened to, but to disburthen my heart of the witness I have to bear, that I may be free to go back to my garden lawns, and paint birds and flowers there.

70. For these same statutes which we are to consider to-day, have indeed been in my mind

now these fourteen years, ever since I wrote the last volume of the 'Stones of Venice,' in which you will find, in the long note on Modern Education, most of what I have been now in detail writing to you, hinted in abstract; and, at the close of it, this sentence, of which I solemnly now avouch (in thankfulness that I was permitted to write it), every word: "Finally, I hold it for indisputable, that the first duty of a State is to see that every child born therein shall be well housed, clothed, fed, and educated, till it attain years of discretion. But in order to the effecting this the Government must have an authority over the people of which we now do not so much as dream."

That authority I did not then endeavour to define, for I knew all such assertions would be useless, and that the necessarily resultant outcry would merely diminish my influence in other directions. But now I do not care about influence any more, it being only my concern to say truly that which I know, and, if it may be, get some quiet life, yet, among the fields in the evening shadow.

71. There is, I suppose, no word which men are prouder of the right to attach to their names,

or more envious of others who bear it, when they themselves may not, than the word "noble." Do you know what it originally meant, and always, in the right use of it, means? It means a "known" person; one who has risen far enough above others to draw men's eyes to him, and to be known (honourably) for such and such an one. "Ignoble," on the other hand, is derived from the same root as the word "ignorance." It means an unknown, inglorious person. And no more singular follies have been committed by weak human creatures than those which have been caused by the instinct, pure and simple, of escaping from this obscurity. Instinct, which, corrupted, will hesitate at no means, good or evil, of satisfying itself with notoriety—instinct, nevertheless, which, like all other natural ones, has a true and pure purpose, and ought always in a worthy way to be satisfied.

All men ought to be in this sense "noble"; known of each other, and desiring to be known. And the first law which a nation, desiring to conquer all the devices of the Father of Lies, should establish among its people, is that they *shall* be so known.

72. Will you please now read § 22 of 'Sesame

and Lilies'? The reviewers in the ecclesiastical journals laughed at it, as a rhapsody, when the book came out; none having the slightest notion of what I meant: (nor, indeed, do I well see how it could be otherwise!). Nevertheless, I meant precisely and literally what is there said, namely, that a bishop's duty being to watch over the souls of his people, and *give* account of every one of them, it becomes practically necessary for him first to *get* some account of their bodies. Which he was wont to do in the early days of Christianity by help of a person called "deacon" or "ministering servant," whose name is still retained among preliminary ecclesiastical dignities, vainly enough! Putting, however, all question of forms and names aside, the thing actually needing to be done is this—that over every hundred (more or less) of the families composing a Christian State, there should be appointed an overseer, or bishop, to render account, to the State, of the life of every individual in those families; and to have care both of their interest and conduct to such an extent as they may be willing to admit, or as their faults may justify: so that it may be impossible for any person, however humble, to suffer from unknown want, or live in unrecognised crime; —such help and observance being rendered without officiousness either of interference or inquisition (the limits of both being determined by national law), but with the patient and gentle watchfulness which true Christian pastors now exercise over their flocks; only with a higher legal authority presently to be defined, of interference on due occasion.

And with this farther function, that such overseers shall be not only the pastors, but the biographers, of their people; a written statement of the principal events in the life of each family being annually required to be rendered by them to a superior State Officer. These records, laid up in public offices, would soon furnish indications of the families whom it would be advantageous to the nation to advance in position, or distinguish with honour, and aid by such reward as it should be the object of every Government to distribute no less punctually, and far more frankly, than it distributes punishment: (compare 'Munera Pulveris,' Essay IV., in paragraph on Critic Law), while the mere fact of permanent record being kept of every event of importance, whether disgraceful or worthy of praise, in each family, would of itself be a deterrent from crime, and a stimulant to well-deserving conduct, far beyond mere punishment or reward.

73. Nor need you think that there would be anything in such a system un-English, or tending to espionage. No uninvited visits should ever be made in any house, unless law had been violated; nothing recorded, against its will, of any family, but what was inevitably known of its publicly visible conduct, and the results of that conduct. What else was written should be only by the desire, and from the communications, of its head. And in a little while it would come to be felt that the true history of a nation was indeed not of its wars, but of its households; and the desire of men would rather be to obtain some conspicuous place in these honourable annals, than to shrink behind closed shutters from public sight. Until at last, George Herbert's grand word of command would hold not only on the conscience, but the actual system and outer economy of life,

"Think the King sees thee still, for *his* King does."

74. Secondly, above these bishops or pastors, who are only to be occupied in offices of

familiar supervision and help, should be appointed higher officers of State, having executive authority over as large districts as might be conveniently (according to the number and circumstances of their inhabitants) committed to their care ; officers who, according to the reports of the pastors, should enforce or mitigate the operation of too rigid general law, and determine measures exceptionally necessary for public advantage. For instance, the general law being that all children of the operative classes, at a certain age, should be sent to public schools, these superior officers should have power, on the report of the pastors, to dispense with the attendance of children who had sick parents to take charge of, or whose home-life seemed to be one of better advantage for them than that of the common schools ; or who, for any other like cause, might justifiably claim remission. And it being the general law that the entire body of the public should contribute to the cost, and divide the profits, of all necessary public works and undertakings, as roads, mines, harbour protections, and the like, and that nothing of this kind should be permitted to be in the hands of private speculators, it should be the duty of the district officer to collect whatever information was accessible respecting such sources of public profit; and to represent the circumstances in Parliament: and then, with Parliamentary authority, but on his own sole personal responsibility, to see that such enterprises were conducted honestly, and with due energy and order.

The appointment to both these offices should be by election, and for life; by what forms of election shall be matter of inquiry, after we have determined some others of the necessary constitutional laws.

75. I do not doubt but that you are already beginning to think it was with good reason I held my peace these fourteen years,—and that, for any good likely to be done by speaking, I might as well have held it altogether!

It may be so: but merely to complete and explain my own work, it is necessary that I should say these things finally; and I believe that the imminent danger to which we are now in England exposed by the gradually accelerated fall of our aristocracy (wholly their own fault), and the substitution of money-power for their martial one; and by the correspondingly imminent prevalence of mob violence here, as in America; together with the continually increasing chances of insane war, founded on popular passion, whether of pride, fear, or acquisitiveness,—all these dangers being further darkened and degraded by the monstrous forms of vice and selfishness which the appliances of recent wealth, and of vulgar mechanical art, make possible to the million,—will soon bring us into a condition in which men will be glad to listen to almost any words but those of a demagogue, and to seek any means of safety rather than those in which they have lately trusted. So, with your good leave, I will say my say to the end, mock at it who may.

P.S.—I take due note of the regulations of trade proposed in your letter just received*—all excellent. I shall come to them presently, "Cash payment" above all. You may write that on your trade-banners in letters of gold, wherever you would have them raised victoriously.

* Appendix 6.

LETTER XIV.

The First Group of Essential Laws—Against Theft by False Work, and by Bankruptcy. —Necessary Publicity of Accounts.

March 26, 1867.

76. I FEEL much inclined to pause at this point, to answer the kind of questions and objections which I know must be rising in your mind, respecting the authority supposed to be lodged in the persons of the officers just specified. But I can neither define, nor justify to you, the powers I would desire to see given to them, till I state to you the kind of laws they would have to enforce: of which the first group should be directed to the prevention of all kinds of thieving; but chiefly of the occult and polite methods of it; and, of all occult methods, chiefly, the making and selling of bad goods. No form of theft is so criminal as this —none so deadly to the State. If you break into a man's house and steal a hundred pounds' worth of plate, he knows his loss, and there

is an end (besides that you take your risk of punishment for your gain, like a man). And if you do it bravely and openly, and habitually live by such inroad, you may retain nearly every moral and manly virtue, and become a heroic rider and reiver, and hero of song. But if you swindle me out of twenty shillings' worth of quality on each of a hundred bargains, I lose my hundred pounds all the same, and I get a hundred untrustworthy articles besides, which will fail me and injure me in all manner of ways, when I least expect it; and you, having done your thieving basely, are corrupted by the guilt of it to the very heart's core.

77. This is the first thing, therefore, which your general laws must be set to punish, fiercely, immitigably, to the utter prevention and extinction of it, or there is no hope for you. No religion that ever was preached on this earth of God's rounding ever proclaimed any salvation to sellers of bad goods. If the Ghost that is in you, whatever the essence of it, leaves your hand a juggler's, and your heart a cheat's, it is not a Holy Ghost, be assured of that. And for the rest, all political economy, as well as all higher virtue, depends *first on sound work*.

Let your laws, then, I say, in the beginning, be set to secure this. You cannot make punishment too stern for subtle knavery. Keep no truce with this enemy, whatever pardon you extend to more generous ones. For light weights and false measures, or for proved adulteration or dishonest manufacture of article, the penalty should be simply confiscation of goods and sending out of the country. The kind of person who desires prosperity by such practices could not be made to "emigrate" too speedily. What to do with him in the place you appointed to be blessed by his presence, we will in time consider.

78. Under such penalty, however, and yet more under the pressure of such a right public opinion as could pronounce and enforce such penalty, I imagine that sham articles would become speedily as rare as sound ones are now. The chief difficulty in the matter would be to fix your standard. This would have to be done by the guild of every trade in its own manner, and within certain easily recognisable limits, and this fixing of standard would necessitate much simplicity in the forms and kinds of articles sold. You could only warrant a certain kind of glazing or painting in china, a certain

quality of leather or cloth, bricks of a certain clay, loaves of a defined mixture of meal. Advisable improvements or varieties in manufacture would have to be examined and accepted by the trade guild: when so accepted, they would be announced in public reports; and all puffery and self-proclamation, on the part of tradesmen, absolutely forbidden, as much as the making of any other kind of noise or disturbance.

79. But observe, this law is only to have force over tradesmen whom I suppose to have joined voluntarily in carrying out a better system of commerce. Outside of their guild, they would have to leave the rogue to puff and cheat as he chose, and the public to be gulled as they chose. All that is necessary is that the said public should clearly know the shops in which they could get warranted articles; and, as clearly, those in which they bought at their own risk.

And the above-named penalty of confiscation of goods should of course be enforced only against dishonest members of the trade guild. If people chose to buy of those who had openly refused to join an honest society, they should be permitted to do so, at their pleasure, and peril: and this for two reasons,—the first, that

XIV. TRADE-WARRANT.

it is always necessary, in enacting strict law, to leave some safety valve for outlet of irrepressible vice (nearly all the stern lawgivers of old time erred by oversight in this; so that the morbid elements of the State, which it should be allowed to get rid of in a cutaneous and openly curable manner, were thrown inwards, and corrupted its constitution, and broke all down);—the second, that operations of trade and manufacture conducted under, and guarded by, severe law, ought always to be subject to the stimulus of such erratic external ingenuity as cannot be tested by law, or would be hindered from its full exercise by the dread of it; not to speak of the farther need of extending all possible indulgence to foreign traders who might wish to exercise their industries here without liability to the surveillance of our trade guilds.

80. Farther, while for all articles warranted by the guild (as above supposed) the prices should be annually fixed for the trade throughout the kingdom; and the producing workman's wages fixed, so as to define the master's profits within limits admitting only such variation as the nature of the given article of sale rendered inevitable;—yet, in the production of

other classes of articles, whether by skill of applied handicraft, or fineness of material above the standard of the guild, attaining, necessarily, values above its assigned prices, every firm should be left free to make its own independent efforts and arrangements with its workmen, subject always to the same penalty, if it could be proved to have consistently described, or offered, anything to the public for what it was not: and finally, the state of the affairs of every firm should be annually reported to the guild, and its books laid open to inspection, for guidance in the regulation of prices in the subsequent year; and any firm whose liabilities exceeded its assets by a hundred pounds should be forthwith declared bankrupt. And I will anticipate what I have to say in succeeding letters so far as to tell you that I would have this condition extend to every firm in the country, large or small, and of whatever rank in business. And thus you perceive, my friend, I shall not have to trouble you or myself much with deliberations respecting commercial "panics," nor to propose legislative cures for *them*, by any laxatives or purgatives of paper currency, or any other change of pecuniary diet.

LETTER XV.

The Nature of Theft by Unjust Profits.—Crime can finally be arrested only by Education.

29th March.

81. THE first methods of polite robbery, by dishonest manufacture and by debt, of which we have been hitherto speaking, are easily enough to be dealt with and ended, when once men have a mind to end them. But the third method of polite robbery, by dishonest *acquisition*, has many branches, and is involved among honest arts of acquisition, so that it is difficult to repress the one without restraining the other.

Observe, first, large fortunes cannot honestly be made by the work of any *one* man's hands or head. If his work benefits multitudes, and involves position of high trust, it may be (I do not say that it *is*) expedient to reward him with great wealth or estate; but fortune of this kind is freely given in gratitude for benefit, not as repayment for labour. Also, men of peculiar genius in any art, if the public can enjoy the product of their genius, may set it at almost any price they choose; but this, I will show you when I come to speak of art, is unlawful on their part, and ruinous to their own powers. Genius must not be sold; the sale of it involves, in a transcendental, but perfectly true, sense, the guilt both of simony and prostitution. Your labour only may be sold; your soul must not.

82. Now, by fair pay for fair labour, according to the rank of it, a man can obtain means of comfortable, or if he needs it, refined life. But he cannot obtain large fortune. Such fortunes as are now the prizes of commerce can be made only in one of three ways:—

(1.) By obtaining command over the labour of multitudes of other men, and taxing it for our own profit.

(2.) By treasure-trove,—as of mines, useful vegetable products, and the like,—in circumstances putting them under our own exclusive control.

(3.) By speculation, (commercial gambling).

The first two of these means of obtaining riches are, in some forms and within certain limits, lawful, and advantageous to the State. The third is entirely detrimental to it; for in all cases of profit derived from speculation, at best, what one man gains another loses; and the net result to the State is zero, (pecuniarily,) with the loss of the time and ingenuity spent in the transaction; besides the disadvantage involved in the discouragement of the losing party, and the corrupted moral natures of both. This is the result of speculation at its best. At its worst, not only B loses what A gains (having taken his fair risk of such loss for his fair chance of gain), but C and D, who never had any chance at all, are drawn in by B's fall, and the final result is that A sets up his carriage on the collected sum which was once the means of living to a dozen families.

83. Nor is this all. For while real commerce is founded on real necessities or uses, and limited by these, speculation, of which the object is merely gain, seeks to excite imaginary necessities and popular desires, in order to gather its temporary profit from the supply of them. So that not only the persons who lend

their money to it will be finally robbed, but the work done with their money will be, for the most part, useless, and thus the entire body of the public injured as well as the persons concerned in the transaction. Take, for instance, the architectural decorations of railways throughout the kingdom,—representing many millions of money for which no farthing of dividend can ever be forthcoming. The public will not be induced to pay the smallest fraction of higher fare to Rochester or Dover because the ironwork of the bridge which carries them over the Thames is covered with floral cockades, and the piers of it edged with ornamental cornices. All that work is simply put there by the builders that they may put the percentage upon it into their own pockets; and, the rest of the money being thrown into that floral form, there is an end of it, as far as the shareholders are concerned. Millions upon millions have thus been spent, within the last twenty years, on ornamental arrangements of zigzag bricks, black and blue tiles, cast-iron foliage, and the like; of which millions, as I said, not a penny can ever return into the shareholders' pockets, nor contribute to public speed or safety on the line. It is all sunk for ever in ornamental architecture, and (trust me for this!) *all that architecture is bad.* As such, it had incomparably better not have been built. Its only result will be to corrupt what capacity of taste or right pleasure in·such work we have yet left to us! And consider a little, what other kind of result than that might have been attained if all those millions had been spent usefully: say, in buying land for the people, or building good houses for them, or (if it had been imperatively required to be spent decoratively) in laying out gardens and parks for them,—or buying noble works of art for their permanent possession,—or, best of all, establishing frequent public schools and libraries. Count what those lost millions would have so accomplished for you! But you left the affair to "supply and demand," and the British public had not brains enough to "demand" land, or lodging, or books. It "demanded" cast-iron cockades and zigzag cornices, and is "supplied" with them, to its beatitude for evermore.

84. Now, the theft we first spoke of, by falsity of workmanship or material, is, indeed, so far worse than these thefts by dishonest

acquisition, that there is no possible excuse for it on the ground of self-deception; while many speculative thefts are committed by persons who really mean to do no harm, but think the system on the whole a fair one, and do the best they can in it for themselves. But in the real fact of the crime, when consciously committed, in the numbers reached by its injury, in the degree of suffering it causes to those whom it ruins, in the baseness of its calculated betrayal of implicit trust, in the yet more perfect vileness of the obtaining such trust by misrepresentation, only that it *may* be betrayed, and in the impossibility that the crime should be at all committed, except by persons of good position and large knowledge of the world—what manner of theft is so wholly unpardonable, so inhuman, so contrary to every law and instinct which binds or animates society?

And then consider farther, how many of the carriages that glitter in our streets are driven, and how many of the stately houses that gleam among our English fields are inhabited, by this kind of thief!

85. I happened to be reading this morning (29th March) some portions of the Lent services

and I came to a pause over the familiar words, "And with Him they crucified two thieves." Have you ever considered (I speak to you now as a professing Christian), why, in the accomplishment of the "numbering among transgressors," the transgressors chosen should have been especially thieves—not murderers, nor, as far as we know, sinners by any gross violence? Do you observe how the sin of theft is again and again indicated as the chiefly antagonistic one to the law of Christ? "This he said, not that he cared for the poor, but because he was a thief, and had the bag" (of Judas). And again, though Barabbas was a leader of sedition, and a murderer besides,—(that the popular election might be in all respects perfect)—yet St. John, in curt and conclusive account of him, fastens again on the theft. "Then cried they all again saying, Not this man, but Barabbas. Now Barabbas was a robber." I believe myself the reason to be that theft is indeed, in its subtle forms, the most complete and excuseless of human crimes. Sins of violence usually are committed under sudden or oppressive temptation: they may be the madness of moments; or they may be apparently the only means of extrication from calamity. In other cases, they are the diseased acts or habits of lower and brutified natures.* But theft involving deliberative intellect, and absence of passion, is the purest type of wilful iniquity, in persons capable of doing right. Which being so, it seems to be fast becoming the practice of modern society to crucify its Christ indeed, as willingly as ever, in the persons of His poor; but by no means now to crucify its thieves beside Him! It elevates its thieves after another fashion; sets them upon a hill, that their light may shine before men and that all may see their good works, and glorify their Father, in—the Opposite of Heaven.

86. I think your trade parliament will have to put an end to this kind of business somehow! But it cannot be done by laws merely, where the interests and circumstances are so extended and complex. Nay, even as regards lower and more defined crimes, the assigned punishment is not to be thought of as a preventive means; but only as the seal of opinion set by society on the fact. Crime cannot be

* [See the analysis of the moral system of Dante, respecting punishment, given in 'Fors Clavigera,' Letter XXIII.]

hindered by punishment; it will always find some shape and outlet, unpunishable or unclosed. Crime can only be truly hindered by letting no man grow up a criminal—by taking away the *will* to commit sin; not by mere punishment of its commission. Crime, small and great, can only be truly stayed by education—not the education of the intellect only, which is, on some men, wasted, and for others mischievous; but education of the heart, which is alike good and necessary for all. So, on this matter, I will try in my next letter to say one or two things of which the silence has kept my own heart heavy this many a day.

LETTER XVI.

Of Public Education irrespective of Class-distinction. It consists essentially in giving Habits of Mercy, and Habits of Truth. (Gentleness* and Justice.)

March 30th, 1867.

87. THANK you for sending me the pamphlet containing the account of the meeting of clergy and workmen, and of the reasonings which there took place. I cannot promise you that I shall read much of them, for the question to my mind most requiring discussion and explanation is not, why workmen don't go to church, but—why other people do. However, this I know, that if among our many spiritual teachers, there are indeed any who heartily and literally believe that the wisdom they have to teach "is more precious than rubies, and all the things thou canst desire are

---

* "Mercy," in its full sense, means delight in perceiving nobleness, or in doing kindness. Compare § 50.

not to be compared unto her," and if, so believing, they will further dare to affront their congregations by the assertion; and plainly tell them they are not to hunt for rubies or gold any more, at their peril, till they have gained that which cannot be gotten for gold, nor silver weighed for the price thereof,—such believers, so preaching, and refusing to preach otherwise till they are in that attended to, will never want congregations, both of working men, and every other kind of men.

88. Did you ever hear of anything else so ill-named as the phantom called the "Philosopher's Stone"? A talisman that shall turn base metal into precious metal, nature acknowledges not; nor would any but fools seek after it. But a talisman to turn base souls into noble souls, nature has given us! and that is a "Philosopher's Stone" indeed, but it is a stone which the builders refuse.

89. If there were two valleys in California or Australia, with two different kinds of gravel in the bottom of them; and in the one stream bed you could dig up, occasionally and by good fortune, nuggets of gold; and in the other stream bed, certainly and without hazard, you could

dig up little caskets, containing talismans which gave length of days and peace; and alabaster vases of precious balms, which were better than the Arabian Dervish's ointment, and made not only the eyes to see, but the mind to know, whatever it would—I wonder in which of the stream beds there would be most diggers?

90. "Time is money"—so say your practised merchants and economists. None of them, however, I fancy, as they draw towards death, find that the reverse is true, and that "money is time"? Perhaps it might be better for them, in the end, if they did not turn so much of their time into money, lest, perchance, they also turn Eternity into it! There are other things, however, which in the same sense are money, or can be changed into it, as well as time. Health is money, wit is money, knowledge is money; and all your health, and wit, and knowledge may be changed for gold; and the happy goal so reached, of a sick, insane, and blind, auriferous old age; but the gold cannot be changed in its turn back into health and wit.

91. "Time is money;" the words tingle in my ears so that I can't go on writing. Is it nothing better, then? If we could thoroughly

understand that time was—*itself*,—would it not be more to the purpose? A thing of which loss or gain was absolute loss, and perfect gain. And that it was expedient also to buy health and knowledge with money, if so purchaseable; but not to buy money with *them?*

And purchaseable they are at the beginning of life, though not at its close. Purchaseable, always, for others, if not for ourselves. You can buy, and cheaply, life, endless life, according to your Christian's creed—(there's a bargain for you!) but—long years of knowledge, and peace, and power, and happiness of love—these assuredly and irrespectively of any creed or question,—for all those desolate and haggard children about your streets.

92. "That is not political economy, however." Pardon me; the all-comfortable saying, "What he layeth out, it shall be paid him again," is quite literally true in matters of education; no money seed can be sown with so sure and large return at harvest-time as that; only of this money-seed, more than of flesh-seed, it is utterly true, "That which thou sowest is not quickened except it *die.*" You must forget your money, and every other material

interest, and educate for education's sake only! or the very good you try to bestow will become venomous, and that and your money will be lost together.

93. And this has been the real cause of failure in our efforts for education hitherto—whether from above or below. There is no honest desire for the thing itself. The cry for it among the lower orders is because they think that, when once they have got it, they must become upper orders. There is a strange notion in the mob's mind now-a-days (including all our popular economists and educators, as we most justly may, under that brief term "mob"), that *everybody* can be uppermost; or at least, that a state of general scramble, in which everybody in his turn should come to the top, is a proper Utopian constitution; and that, once give every lad a good education, and he cannot but come to ride in his carriage (the methods of supply of coachmen and footmen not being contemplated). And very sternly I say to you—and say from sure knowledge—that a man had better not know how to read and write, than receive education on such terms.

94. The first condition under which it can

be given usefully is, that it should be clearly understood to be no means of getting on in the world, but a means of staying pleasantly in your place there. And the first elements of State education should be calculated equally for the advantage of every order of person composing the State. From the lowest to the highest class, every child born in this island should be required by law to receive these general elements of human discipline, and to be baptized—not with a drop of water on its forehead—but in the cloud and sea of heavenly wisdom and of earthly power.

And the elements of this general State education should be briefly these:

95. First—The body must be made as beautiful and perfect in its youth as it can be, wholly irrespective of ulterior purpose. If you mean afterwards to set the creature to business which will degrade its body and shorten its life, first, I should say, simply,—you had better let such business alone;—but if you must have it done, somehow, yet let the living creature, whom you mean to kill, get the full strength of its body first, and taste the joy, and bear the beauty of youth. After that, poison it, if you will.

Economically, the arrangement is a wiser one, for it will take longer in the killing than if you began with it younger; and you will get an excess of work out of it which will more than pay for its training.

Therefore, first teach—as I have said in the preface to 'Unto this Last'—"The Laws of Health, and exercises enjoined by them;" and, to this end, your schools must be in fresh country, and amidst fresh air, and have great extents of land attached to them in permanent estate. Riding, running, all the honest, personal exercises of offence and defence, and music, should be the primal heads of this bodily education.

96. Next to these bodily accomplishments, the two great mental graces should be taught, Reverence and Compassion: not that these are in a literal sense to be "taught," for they are innate in every well-born human creature, but they have to be developed exactly as the strength of the body must be, by deliberate and constant exercise. I never understood why Goethe (in the plan of education in 'Wilhelm Meister') says that reverence is not innate, but must be taught from without; it seems to me

so fixedly a function of the human spirit, that if men can get nothing else to reverence they will worship a fool, or a stone, or a vegetable.* But to teach reverence rightly is to attach it to the right persons and things; first, by setting over your youth masters whom they cannot but love and respect; next, by gathering for them, out of past history, whatever has been most worthy in human deeds and human passion; and leading them continually to dwell upon such instances, making this the principal element of emotional excitement to them; and, lastly, by letting them justly feel, as far as may be, the smallness of their own powers and knowledge, as compared with the attainments of others.

97. Compassion, on the other hand, is to be taught chiefly by making it a point of honour, collaterally with courage, and in the same rank (as indeed the complement and evidence of courage), so that, in the code of unwritten school law, it shall be held as shameful to have done a cruel thing as a cowardly one. All infliction of pain on weaker creatures is to be

---

* By steady preaching against it, one may quench reverence, and bring insolence to its height; but the instinc cannot be wholly uprooted.

stigmatized as unmanly crime; and every possible opportunity taken to exercise the youths in offices of some practical help, and to acquaint them with the realities of the distress which, in the joyfulness of entering into life, it is so difficult, for those who have not seen home suffering, to conceive.

98. Reverence, then, and compassion, we are to teach primarily, and with these, as the bond and guardian of them, truth of spirit and word, of thought and sight. Truth, earnest and passionate, sought for like a treasure, and kept like a crown.

This teaching of truth as a habit will be the chief work the master has to do; and it will enter into all parts of education. First, you must accustom the children to close accuracy of statement; this both as a principle of honour, and as an accomplishment of language, making them try always who shall speak truest, both as regards the fact he has to relate or express (not concealing or exaggerating), and as regards the precision of the words he expresses it in, thus making truth (which, indeed, it is) the test of perfect language, and giving the intensity of a moral purpose to the study and art of words: then carrying this accuracy into all habits of thought and observation also, so as always to *think* of things as they truly are, and to *see* them as they truly are, as far as in us rests. And it does rest much in our power, for all false thoughts and seeings come mainly of our thinking of what we have no business with, and looking for things we want to see, instead of things that ought to be seen.

99. "Do not talk but of what you know; do not think but of what you have materials to think justly upon; and do not look for things only that you like, when there are others to be seen"—this is the lesson to be taught to our youth, and inbred in them; and that mainly by our own example and continence. Never teach a child anything of which you are not yourself sure; and, above all, if you feel anxious to force anything into its mind in tender years, that the virtue of youth and early association may fasten it there, be sure it is no lie which you thus sanctify. There is always more to be taught of absolute, incontrovertible knowledge, open to its capacity, than any child can learn; there is no need to teach it anything doubtful. Better that it should be ignorant of

a thousand truths, than have consecrated in its heart a single lie.

100. And for this, as well as for many other reasons, the principal subjects of education, after history, ought to be natural science and mathematics; but with respect to these studies, your schools will require to be divided into three groups: one for children who will probably have to live in cities, one for those who will live in the country, and one for those who will live at sea; the schools for these last, of course, being always placed on the coast. And for children whose life is to be in cities, the subjects of study should be, as far as their disposition will allow of it, mathematics and the arts; for children who are to live in the country, natural history of birds, insects, and plants, together with agriculture taught practically; and for children who are to be seamen, physical geography, astronomy, and the natural history of sea fish and sea birds.

101. This, then, being the general course and material of education for all children, observe farther, that in the preface to 'Unto this Last' I said that every child, besides passing through this course, was at school to learn "the calling

by which it was to live." And it may perhaps appear to you that after, or even in the early stages of education such as this above described, there are many callings which, however much called to them, the children might not willingly determine to learn or live by. "Probably," you may say, "after they have learned to ride, and fence, and sing, and know birds and flowers, it will be little to their liking to make themselves into tailors, carpenters, shoemakers, blacksmiths, and the like." And I cannot but agree with you as to the exceeding probability of some such reluctance on their part, which will be a very awkward state of things indeed, (since we can by no means get on without tailoring and shoe-making,) and one to be meditated upon very seriously in next letter.

102. P.S.—Thank you for sending me your friend's letter about Gustave Doré; he is wrong, however, in thinking there is any good in those illustrations of 'Elaine.' I had intended to speak of them afterwards, for it is to my mind quite as significant—almost as awful—a sign of what is going on in the midst of us, that our great English poet should have suffered his work to be thus contaminated, as that the lower

Evangelicals, never notable for sense in the arts, should have got their Bibles dishonoured. Those 'Elaine' illustrations are just as impure as anything else that Doré has done; but they are also vapid, and without any one merit whatever in point of art. The illustrations to the 'Contes Drôlatiques' are full of power and invention; but those to 'Elaine' are merely and simply stupid; theatrical bêtises, with the taint of the charnel-house on them besides.

LETTER XVII.

The Relations of Education to Position in Life.

April 3, 1867.

103. I AM not quite sure that you will feel the awkwardness of the dilemma I got into at the end of last letter, as much I do myself. You working men have been crowing and peacocking at such a rate lately; and setting yourselves forth so confidently for the cream of society, and the top of the world, that perhaps you will not anticipate any of the difficulties which suggest themselves to a thoroughbred Tory and Conservative, like me. Perhaps you will expect a youth properly educated— a good rider—musician—and well-grounded scholar in natural philosophy, to think it a step of promotion when he has to go and be made a tailor of, or a coalheaver? If you do, I should very willingly admit that you might be right, and go on to the farther development of my

notions without pausing at this stumbling-block, were it not that, unluckily, all the wisest men whose sayings I ever heard or read, agree in expressing (one way or another) just such contempt for those useful occupations, as I dread on the part of my foolishly refined scholars. Shakespeare and Chaucer,—Dante and Virgil,—Horace and Pindar,—Homer, Æschylus, and Plato,—all the men of any age or country who seem to have had Heaven's music on their lips, agree in their scorn of mechanic life. And I imagine that the feeling of prudent Englishmen, and sensible as well as sensitive Englishwomen, on reading my last letter, would mostly be—"Is the man mad, or laughing at us, to propose educating the working classes this way? He could not, if his wild scheme were possible, find a better method of making them acutely wretched."

104. It may be so, my sensible and polite friends; and I am heartily willing, as well as curious, to hear you develop your own scheme of operative education, so only that it be universal, orderly, and careful. I do not say that I shall be prepared to advocate my athletics and philosophies instead. Only, observe what you

admit, or imply, in bringing forward your possibly wiser system. You imply that a certain portion of mankind must be employed in degrading work; and that, to fit them for this work, it is necessary to limit their knowledge, their active powers, and their enjoyments, from childhood upwards, so that they may not be able to conceive of any state better than the one they were born in, nor possess any knowledge or acquirements inconsistent with the coarseness, or disturbing the monotony, of their vulgar occupation. And by their labour in this contracted state of mind, we superior beings are to be maintained; and always to be curtseyed to by the properly ignorant little girls, and capped by the properly ignorant little boys, whenever we pass by.

105. Mind, I do not say that this is *not* the right state of things. Only, if it be, you need not be so over-particular about the slave-trade, it seems to me. What is the use of arguing so pertinaciously that a black's skull will hold as much as a white's, when you are declaring in the same breath that a white's skull must not hold as much as it can, or it will be the worse for him? It does not appear to me at all a

profound state of slavery to be whipped into doing a piece of low work that I don't like; but it is a very profound state of slavery to be kept, myself, low in the forehead, that I may not dislike low work.

106. You see, my friend, the dilemma is really an awkward one, whichever way you look at it. But, what is still worse, I am not puzzled only, at this part of my scheme, about the boys I shall have to make *workmen* of; I am just as much puzzled about the boys I shall have to make *nothing* of! Grant, that by hook or crook, by reason or rattan, I persuade a certain number of the roughest ones into some serviceable business, and get coats and shoes made for the rest, —what is the business of "the rest" to be? Naturally, according to the existing state of things, one supposes they are to belong to some of the gentlemanly professions; to be soldiers, lawyers, doctors, or clergymen. But alas, I shall not want any soldiers of special skill or pugnacity. *All* my boys will be soldiers. So far from wanting any lawyers, of the kind that live by talking, I shall have the strongest possible objection to their appearance in the country. For doctors, I shall always entertain a profound

respect; but when I get my athletic education fairly established, of what help to them will my respect be? They will all starve! And for clergymen, it is true, I shall have a large number of episcopates—one over every hundred families—(and many positions of civil authority also, for civil officers, above them and below), but all these places will involve much hard work, and be anything but covetable; while, of clergymen's usual work, admonition, theological demonstration, and the like, I shall want very little done indeed, and that little done for nothing! for I will allow no man to admonish anybody, until he has previously earned his own dinner by more productive work than admonition.

Well, I wish, my friend, you would write me a word or two in answer to this, telling me your own ideas as to the proper issue out of these difficulties. I should like to know what you think, and what you suppose others will think, before I tell you my own notions about the matter.

LETTER XVIII.

The harmful Effects of Servile Employments. The possible Practice and Exhibition of sincere Humility by Religious Persons.

April 7, 1867.

107. I HAVE been waiting these three days to know what you would say to my last questions; and now you send me two pamphlets of Combe's to read! I never read anything in spring-time (except the Ai, Ai, on the "sanguine flower inscribed with woe"); and, besides, if, as I gather from your letter, Combe thinks that among well-educated boys there would be a percentage constitutionally inclined to be cobblers, or looking forward with unction to establishment in the oil and tallow line, or fretting themselves for a flunkey's uniform, nothing that he could say would make me agree with him. I know, as well as he does, the unconquerable differences in the clay of the human creature: and I know that, in the outset,

whatever system of education you adopted, a large number of children could be made nothing of, and would necessarily fall out of the ranks, and supply candidates enough for degradation to common mechanical business: but this enormous difference in bodily and mental capacity has been mainly brought about by difference in occupation, and by direct maltreatment; and in a few generations, if the poor were cared for, their marriages looked after, and sanitary law enforced, a beautiful type of face and form, and a high intelligence, would become all but universal, in a climate like this of England. Even as it is, the marvel is always to me, how the race resists, at least in its childhood, influences of ill-regulated birth, poisoned food, poisoned air, and soul neglect. I often see faces of children, as I walk through the black district of St. Giles's (lying, as it does, just between my own house and the British Museum), which, through all their pale and corrupt misery, recall the old "Non Angli," and recall it, not by their beauty, but by their sweetness of expression, even though signed already with trace and cloud of the coming life,—a life so bitter that it would make the curse of the 137th Psalm true upon our modern Babylon, though we were to read it thus, "Happy shall *thy children* be, if one taketh and dasheth them against the stones."

108. Yes, very solemnly I repeat to you that in those worst treated children of the English race, I yet see the making of gentlemen and gentlewomen—not the making of dog-stealers and gin-drinkers, such as their parents were; and the child of the average English tradesman or peasant, even at this day, well schooled, will show no innate disposition such as must fetter him for ever to the clod or the counter. You say that many a boy runs away, or would run away if he could, from good positions to go to sea. Of course he does. I never said I should have any difficulty in finding sailors, but I shall in finding fishmongers. I am at no loss for gardeners either, but what am I to do for greengrocers?

109. The fact is, a great number of quite necessary employments are, in the accuratest sense, "Servile;" that is, they sink a man to the condition of a serf, or unthinking worker, the proper state of an animal, but more or less unworthy of men; nay, unholy in some sense, so that a day is made "holy" by the fact of its

being commanded, "Thou shalt do no *servile* work therein." And yet, if undertaken in a certain spirit, such work might be the holiest of all. If there were but a thread or two of sound fibre here and there left in our modern religion, so that the stuff of it would bear a real strain, one might address our two opposite groups of evangelicals and ritualists somewhat after this fashion:—" Good friends, these differences of opinion between you cannot but be painful to your Christian charity, and they are unseemly to us, the profane; and prevent us from learning from you what, perhaps, we ought. But, as we read your Book, we, for our part, gather from it that you might, without danger to your own souls, set an undivided example to us, for the benefit of ours. You, both of you, as far as we understand, agree in the necessity of humility to the perfection of your character. We often hear you, of Calvinistic persuasion, speaking of yourselves as 'sinful dust and ashes,'— would it then be inconsistent with your feelings to make yourselves into 'serviceable' dust and ashes? We observe that of late many of our roads have been hardened and mended with cinders; now, if, in a higher sense, you could allow us to mend the roads of the world with *you* a little, it would be a great proof to us of your sincerity. Suppose, only for a little while, in the present difficulty and distress, you were to make it a test of conversion that a man should regularly give Zaccheus's portion, half his goods, to the poor, and at once adopt some disagreeable and despised, but thoroughly useful, trade? You cannot think that this would finally be to your disadvantage; you doubtless believe the texts, 'He that giveth to the poor lendeth to the Lord,' and 'He that would be chief among you, let him be your servant.' The more you parted with, and the lower you stooped, the greater would be your final reward, and final exaltation. You profess to despise human learning and worldly riches; leave both of these to *us;* undertake for us the illiterate and ill-paid employments which must deprive you of the privileges of society and the pleasures of luxury. You cannot possibly preach your faith so forcibly to the world by any quantity of the finest words, as by a few such simple and painful acts; and over your counters, in honest retail business, you might preach a gospel that would sound in more ears than any that was ever proclaimed over pulpit cushions or tabernacle rails. And, whatever may be your gifts of utterance, you cannot but feel (studying St. Paul's Epistles as carefully as you do) that you might more easily and modestly emulate the practical teaching of the silent Apostle of the Gentiles than the speech or writing of his companion. Amidst the present discomforts of your brethren you may surely, with greater prospect of good to them, seek the title of Sons of Consolation, than of Sons of Thunder, and be satisfied with Barnabas's confession of faith, (if you can reach no farther,) who, 'having land, sold it, and brought the money and laid it at the Apostles' feet.'

110. "To you, on the other hand, gentlemen of the embroidered robe, who neither despise learning nor the arts, we know that sacrifices such as these would be truly painful, and might at first appear inexpedient. But the doctrine of self-mortification is not a new one to you; and we should be sorry to think—we would not, indeed, for a moment dishonour you by thinking —that these melodious chants, and prismatic brightnesses of vitreous pictures, and floral graces of deep-wrought stone, were in any

wise intended for your own poor pleasures, whatever profane attraction they may exercise on more fleshly-minded persons. And as you have certainly received no definite order for the painting, carving, or lighting up of churches, while the temple of the body of so many poor living Christians is so pale, so mis-shapen, and so ill-lighted; but have, on the contrary, received very definite orders for the feeding and clothing of such sad humanity, we may surely ask you, not unreasonably, to humiliate yourselves in the most complete way—not with a voluntary, but a sternly *in*voluntary humility—not with a show of wisdom in will-worship, but with practical wisdom, in all honour, to the satisfying of the flesh; and to associate yourselves in monasteries and convents for the better practice of useful and humble trades. Do not burn any more candles, but mould some; do not paint any more windows, but mend a few where the wind comes in, in winter time, with substantial clear glass and putty. Do not vault any more high roofs, but thatch some low ones; and embroider rather on backs which are turned to the cold, than only on those which are turned to congregations. And you will have your reward afterwards, and attain, with all your flocks thus tended, to a place where you may have as much gold, and painted glass, and singing, as you like."

Thus much, it seems to me, one might say with some hope of acceptance, to any very earnest member of either of our two great religious parties, if, as I say, their faith could stand a strain. I have not, however, based any of my imaginary political arrangements on the probability of its doing so; and I trust only to such general good nature and willingness to help each other, as I presume may be found among men of the world; to whom I should have to make quite another sort of speech, which I will endeavour to set down the heads of, for you, in next letter.

LETTER XIX.

The General Pressure of Excessive and Improper Work, in English Life.

April 10, 1867.

111. I CANNOT go on to-day with the part of my subject I had proposed, for I was disturbed by receiving a letter last night, which I herewith enclose to you, and of which I wish you to print, here following, the parts I have not underlined :—

1, Phene Street, Chelsea, April 8, 1867.

My Dear R———,—

It is long since you have heard of me, and now I ask your patience with me for a little. I have but just returned from the funeral of my dear, dear friend ———, the first artist friend I made in London—a loved and prized one. For years past he had lived in the very humblest way, fighting his battle of life against mean appreciation of his talents, the wants of a rising family, and frequent attacks of illness, crippling him for months at a time, the wolf at the door meanwhile.

But about two years since his prospects brightened * * * and he had but a few weeks since ventured on removal to a larger house. His eldest boy of seventeen years, a very intelligent youth, so strongly desired to be a civil engineer that Mr. ———, not being able to pay the large premium required for his apprenticeship, had been made very glad by the consent of Mr. Penn, of Millwall, to receive him without a premium after the boy should have spent some time at King's College in the study of mechanics. The rest is a sad story. About a fortnight ago Mr. ——— was taken ill, and died last week, the doctors say, of sheer physical exhaustion, not thirty-nine years old, leaving eight young children, and his poor widow expecting her confinement, and so weak and ill as to be incapable of effort. This youth is the eldest, and the other children range downwards to a babe of eighteen months. There is not one who knew him, I believe, that will not give cheerfully, to their ability, for his widow and children ; but such aid will go but a little way in this painful case ; and it would be a real boon to this poor widow if some of her children could be got into an Orphan Asylum. * * *

If you are able to do anything I would send particulars of the age and sex of the children.

I remain, dear Sir, ever obediently yours,

FRED. J. SHIELDS.

P.S.—I ought to say that poor ——— has been quite unable to save, with his large family ; and that they would be utterly destitute now, but for the kindness of some with whom he was professionally connected.

112. Now this case, of which you see the entire authenticity, is, out of the many of which I hear continually, a *notably* sad one only in so

far as the artist in question has died of distress while he was catering for the public amusement. Hardly a week now passes without some such misery coming to my knowledge; and the quantity of pain, and anxiety of daily effort, through the best part of life, ending all at last in utter grief, which the lower middle classes in England are now suffering, is so great that I feel constantly as if I were living in one great churchyard, with people all round me clinging feebly to the edges of the open graves, and calling for help, as they fall back into them, out of sight.

113. Now I want you to observe here, in a definite case, the working of your beautiful modern political economy of "supply and demand." Here is a man who could have "supplied" you with good and entertaining art,—say for fifty good years,—if you had paid him enough for his day's work to find him and his children peacefully in bread. But you like having your prints as cheap as possible—you triumph in the little that your laugh costs—you take all you can get from the man, give the least you can give to him,—and you accordingly kill him at thirty-nine; and thereafter have his children to take care of, or to kill also,

XIX. BROKEN REEDS.

whichever you choose; but, now, observe, you must take care of *them* for nothing, or not at all; and what you might have had good value for, if you had given it when it would have cheered the father's heart, you now can have no return for at all, to yourselves; and what you give to the orphans, if it does not degrade them, at least afflicts, coming, not through their father's hand, its honest earnings, but from strangers.

Observe farther, whatever help the orphans may receive, will not be from the public at all. It will not be from those who profited by their father's labours; it will be chiefly from his fellow-labourers; or from persons whose money would have been beneficially spent in other directions from whence it is drawn away to this need, which ought never to have occurred,—while those who waste their money without doing any service to the public will never contribute one farthing to this distress.

114. Now it is this double fault in the help —that it comes too late, and that the burden of it falls wholly on those who ought least to be charged with it—which would be corrected by that institution of overseers of which I spoke to you in the twelfth of these letters, saying, you

remember, that they were to have farther legal powers, which I did not then specify, but which would belong to them chiefly in the capacity of public almoners, or help-givers, aided by their deacons, the reception of such help, in time of true need, being not held disgraceful, but honourable; since the fact of its reception would be so entirely public that no impostor or idle person could ever obtain it surreptitiously.

115. (11th April.) I was interrupted yesterday, and I am glad of it, for here happens just an instance of the way in which the unjust distribution of the burden of charity is reflected on general interests; I cannot help what taint of ungracefulness you or other readers of these letters may feel that I incur, in speaking, in this instance, of myself. If I could speak with the same accurate knowledge of any one else, most gladly I would; but I also think it right that, whether people accuse me of boasting or not, they should know that I practise what I preach. I had not intended to say what I now shall, but the coming of this letter last night just turns the balance of the decision with me. I enclose it with the other; you see it is one from my bookseller, Mr. Quaritch, offering me Fischer's work

XIX. BROKEN REEDS.

on the *Flora of Java*, and Latour's on *Indian Orchidaceæ*, bound together, for twenty guineas. Now, I am writing a book on botany just now, for young people, chiefly on wild flowers, and I want these two books very much; but I simply cannot afford to buy them, because I sent my last spare twenty guineas to Mr. Shields yesterday for this widow. And though you may think it not the affair of the public that I have not this book on Indian flowers, it is their affair finally, that what I write for them should be founded on as broad knowledge as possible; whatever value my own book may or may not have, it will just be in a given degree worth *less* to them, because of my want of this knowledge.

116. So again—for having begun to speak of myself I will do so yet more frankly—I suppose that when people see my name down for a hundred pounds to the Cruikshank Memorial, and for another hundred to the Eyre Defence Fund, they think only that I have more money than I know what to do with. Well, the giving of those subscriptions simply decides the question whether or no I shall be able to afford a journey to Switzerland this year, in the negative; and

I wanted to go, not only for health's sake, but to examine the junctions of the molasse sandstones and nagelfluh with the Alpine limestone, in order to complete some notes I meant to publish next spring on the geology of the great northern Swiss valley; notes which must now lie by me at least for another year; and I believe this delay (though I say it) will be really something of a loss to the travelling public, for the little essay was intended to explain to them, in a familiar way, the real wonderfulness of their favourite mountain, the Righi; and to give them some amusement in trying to find out where the many-coloured pebbles of it had come from. But it is more important that I should, with some stoutness, assert my respect for the genius and earnest patriotism of Cruikshank, and my much more than disrespect for the Jamaica Committee, than that I should see the Alps this year, or get my essay finished next spring; but I tell you the fact, because I want you to feel how, in thus leaving their men of worth to be assisted or defended only by those who deeply care for them, the public more or less cripple, to their own ultimate disadvantage, just the people who could serve them in other ways; while the speculators and money-seekers, who are only making their profit out of the said public, of course take no part in the help of anybody. And even if the willing bearers could sustain the burden anywise adequately, none of us would complain; but I am certain there is no man, whatever his fortune, who is now engaged in any earnest offices of kindness to these sufferers, especially of the middle class, among his acquaintance, who will not bear me witness that for one we can relieve, we must leave three to perish. I have left three, myself, in the first three months of this year. One was the artist Paul Gray, for whom an appeal was made to me for funds to assist him in going abroad out of the bitter English winter. I had not the means by me, and he died a week afterwards. Another case was that of a widow whose husband had committed suicide, for whom application was made to me at the same time; and the third was a personal friend, to whom I refused a sum which he said would have saved him from bankruptcy. I believe six times as much would not have saved him; however, I refused, and he is ruined.

117. And observe, also, it is not the mere

crippling of my means that I regret. It is the crippling of my temper, and waste of my time. The knowledge of all this distress, even when I can assist it,—much more when I cannot,— and the various thoughts of what I can and cannot, or ought and ought not, to do, are a far greater burden to me than the mere loss of the money. It is peremptorily not my business— it is not my gift, bodily or mentally, to look after other people's sorrow. I have enough of my own; and even if I had not, the sight of pain is not good for me. I don't want to be a bishop. In a most literal and sincere sense, "*nolo episcopari.*" I don't want to be an almoner, nor a counsellor, nor a Member of Parliament, nor a voter for Members of Parliament. (What would Mr. Holyoake say to me if he knew that I have never voted for anybody in my life, and never mean to do so!) I am essentially a painter and a leaf dissector; and my powers of thought are all purely mathematical, seizing ultimate principles only—never accidents; a line is always, to me, length without breadth; it is not a cable or a crowbar; and though I can almost infallibly reason out the final law of anything, if within reach of my industry, I neither care for, nor can trace, the minor exigencies of its daily appliance. So, in every way, I like a quiet life; and I don't like seeing people cry, or die; and should rejoice, more than I can tell you, in giving up the full half of my fortune for the poor, provided I knew that the public would make Lord Overstone also give the half of his, and other people who were independent give the half of theirs; and then set men who were really fit for such office to administer the fund, and answer to us for nobody's perishing innocently; and so leave us all to do what we chose with the rest, and with our days, in peace.

Thus far of the public's fault in the matter. Next, I have a word or two to say of the sufferers' own fault—for much as I pity them, I conceive that none of them *do* perish altogether innocently. But this must be for next letter.

LETTER XX.

Of Improvidence in Marriage in the Middle Classes; and of the advisable Restrictions of it.

April 12, 1867.

118. IT is quite as well, whatever irregularity it may introduce in the arrangement of the general subject, that yonder sad letter warped me away from the broad inquiry, to this speciality, respecting the present distress of the middle classes. For the immediate cause of that distress, in their own imprudence, of which I have to speak to you to-day, is only to be finally vanquished by strict laws, which, though they have been many a year in my mind, I was glad to have a quiet hour of sunshine for the thinking over again, this morning. Sunshine which happily rose cloudless; and allowed me to meditate my tyrannies before breakfast, under the just opened blossoms of my orchard, and assisted by much melodious advice from the

birds; who (my gardener having positive orders never to trouble any of them in anything, or object to their eating even my best pease if they like their flavour) rather now get *into* my way, than out of it, when they see me about the walks; and take me into most of their counsels in nest-building.

119. The letter from Mr. Shields, which interrupted us, reached me, as you see, on the evening of the 9th instant. On the morning of the 10th, I received another, which I herewith forward to you, for verification. It is—characteristically enough—dateless, so you must take the time of its arrival on my word. And substituting M. N. for the name of the boy referred to, and withholding only the address and name of the writer, you see that it may be printed word for word—as follows:—

SIR,—

May I beg for the favour of your presentation to Christ's Hospital for my youngest son, M. N.? I have nine children, and no means to educate them. I ventured to address you, believing that my husband's name is not unknown to you as an artist.

Believe me to remain faithfully yours,

* * *

120. Now this letter is only a typical example

of the entire class of those which, being a governor of Christ's Hospital, I receive, in common with all the other governors, at the rate of about three a day, for a month or six weeks from the date of our names appearing in the printed list of the governors who have presentations for the current year. Having been a governor now some twenty-five years, I have documentary evidence enough to found some general statistics upon; from which there have resulted two impressions on my mind, which I wish here specially to note to you, and I do not doubt but that all the other governors, if you could ask them, would at once confirm what I say. My first impression is, a heavy and sorrowful sense of the general feebleness of intellect of that portion of the British public which stands in need of presentations to Christ's Hospital. This feebleness of intellect is mainly shown in the nearly total unconsciousness of the writers that anybody else may want a presentation, besides themselves. With the exception here and there of a soldier's or a sailor's widow, hardly one of them seems to have perceived the existence of any distress in the world but their own: none know what they are asking for, or imagine, unless as a remote contingency, the possibility of its having been promised at a prior date. The second most distinct impression on my mind, is that the portion of the British public which is in need of presentations to Christ's Hospital considers it a merit to have large families, with or without the means of supporting them!

121. Now it happened also (and remember, all this is strictly true, nor in the slightest particular represented otherwise than as it chanced; though the said chance brought thus together exactly the evidence I wanted for my letter to you)—it happened, I say, that on this same morning of the 10th April, I became accidentally acquainted with a case of quite a different kind: that of a noble girl, who, engaged at sixteen, and having received several advantageous offers since, has remained for ten years faithful to her equally faithful lover; while, their circumstances rendering it, as they rightly considered, unjustifiable in them to think of marriage, each of them simply and happily, aided and cheered by the other's love, discharged the duties of their own separate positions in life.

122. In the nature of things, instances of this kind of noble life remain more or less concealed,

(while imprudence and error proclaim themselves by misfortune,) but they are assuredly not unfrequent in our English homes. Let us next observe the political and national result of these arrangements. You leave your marriages to be settled by "supply and demand," instead of wholesome law. And thus, among your youths and maidens, the improvident, incontinent, selfish, and foolish ones marry, whether you will or not; and beget families of children necessarily inheritors in a great degree of these parental dispositions; and for whom, supposing they had the best dispositions in the world, you have thus provided, by way of educators, the foolishest fathers and mothers you could find; (the only rational sentence in their letters, usually, is the invariable one, in which they declare themselves "incapable of providing for their children's education"). On the other hand, whosoever is wise, patient, unselfish, and pure among your youth, you keep maid or bachelor; wasting their best days of natural life in painful sacrifice, forbidding them their best help and best reward, and carefully excluding their prudence and tenderness from any offices of parental duty.

Is not this a beatific and beautifully sagacious system for a Celestial Empire, such as that of these British Isles?

123. I will not here enter into any statement of the physical laws which it is the province of our physicians to explain; and which are indeed at last so far beginning to be understood, that there is hope of the nation's giving some of the attention to the conditions affecting the race of man, which it has hitherto bestowed only on those which may better its races of cattle.

It is enough, I think, to say here that the beginning of all sanitary and moral law is in the regulation of marriage, and that, ugly and fatal as is every form and agency of licence, no licentiousness is so mortal as licentiousness in marriage.

124. Briefly, then, and in main points, subject in minor ones to such modifications in detail as local circumstances and characters would render expedient, those following are laws such as a prudent nation would institute respecting its marriages. Permission to marry should be the reward held in sight of its youth during the entire latter part of the course of their education; and it should be granted as the national

attestation that the first portion of their lives had been rightly fulfilled. It should not be attainable without earnest and consistent effort, though put within the reach of all who were willing to make such effort; and the granting of it should be a public testimony to the fact, that the youth or maid to whom it was given had lived, within their proper sphere, a modest and virtuous life, and had attained such skill in their proper handicraft, and in arts of household economy, as might give well-founded expectations of their being able honourably to maintain and teach their children.

125. No girl should receive her permission to marry before her seventeenth birthday, nor any youth before his twenty-first; and it should be a point of somewhat distinguished honour with both sexes to gain their permission of marriage in the eighteenth and twenty-second years; and a recognised disgrace not to have gained it at least before the close of their twenty-first and twenty-fourth. I do not mean that they should in any wise hasten actual marriage; but only that they should hold it a point of honour to have the right to marry. In every year there should be two festivals, one on the

first of May, and one at the feast of harvest home in each district, at which festivals their permissions to marry should be given publicly to the maidens and youths who had won them in that half-year; and they should be crowned, the maids by the old French title of Rosières, and the youths, perhaps by some name rightly derived from one supposed signification of the word "bachelor," "laurel fruit," and so led in joyful procession, with music and singing, through the city street or village lane, and the day ended with feasting of the poor.

126. And every bachelor and rosière should be entitled to claim, if they needed it, according to their position in life, a fixed income from the State, for seven years from the day of their marriage, for the setting up of their homes; and, however rich they might be by inheritance, their income should not be permitted to exceed a given sum, proportioned to their rank, for the seven years following that in which they had obtained their permission to marry, but should accumulate in the trust of the State until that seventh year, in which they should be put (on certain conditions) finally in possession of their property; and the men, thus

necessarily not before their twenty-eighth, nor usually later than their thirty-first year, become eligible to offices of State. So that the rich and poor should not be sharply separated in the beginning of the war of life; but the one supported against the first stress of it long enough to enable them, by proper forethought and economy, to secure their footing; and the other trained somewhat in the use of moderate means, before they were permitted to have the command of abundant ones. And of the sources from which these State incomes for the married poor should be supplied, or of the treatment of those of our youth whose conduct rendered it advisable to refuse them permission to marry, I defer what I have to say till we come to the general subjects of taxation and criminal discipline; leaving the proposals made in this letter to bear, for the present, whatever aspect of mere romance and unrealizable vision they probably may, and to most readers, such as they assuredly will. Nor shall I make the slightest effort to redeem them from these imputations; for though there is nothing in all their purport which would not be approved, as in the deepest sense "practical"—by the Spirit of Paradise—

> Which gives to all the self-same bent,
> Whose lives are wise and innocent,"

and though I know that national justice in conduct, and peace in heart, could by no other laws be so swiftly secured, I confess with much *dis*peace of heart, that both justice and happiness have at this day become, in England, "romantic impossibilities."

LETTER XXI.

Of the Dignity of the Four Fine Arts; and of the Proper System of Retail Trade.

April 15, 1867.

127. I RETURN now to the part of the subject at which I was interrupted—the inquiry as to the proper means of finding persons willing to maintain themselves and others by degrading occupations.

That, on the whole, simply manual occupations *are* degrading, I suppose I may assume you to admit; at all events, the fact is so, and I suppose few general readers will have any doubt of it.*

Granting this, it follows as a direct consequence that it is the duty of all persons in

---

* Many of my working readers have disputed this statement eagerly, feeling the good effect of work in themselves; but observe, I only say, *simply* or *totally* manual work; and that, alone, *is* degrading, though often in measure, refreshing, wholesome, and necessary. So it is highly necessary and wholesome to eat sometimes; but degrading to eat all day,

higher stations of life, by every means in their power to diminish their demand for work of such kind, *and to live with as little aid from the lower trades*, as they can possibly contrive.

128. I suppose you see that this conclusion is not a little at variance with received notions on political economy? It is popularly supposed that it benefits a nation to invent a want. But the fact is, that the true benefit is in extinguishing a want—in living with as few wants as possible.

I cannot tell you the contempt I feel for the common writers on political economy, in their stupefied missing of this first principle of all human economy—individual or political—to live, namely, with as few wants as possible, and to waste nothing of what is given you to supply them.

129. This ought to be the first lesson of every rich man's political code. "Sir," his tutor should early say to him, "you are so placed in society,—it may be for your misfortune, it *must*

as to labour with the hands all day. But it is not degrading to think all day—if you can. A highly-bred court lady, rightly interested in politics and literature, is a much finer type of the human creature than a servant of all work, however clever and honest.

be for your trial—that you are likely to be maintained all your life by the labour of other men. You will have to make shoes for nobody, but some one will have to make a great many for you. You will have to dig ground for nobody, but some one will have to dig through every summer's hot day for you. You will build houses and make clothes for no one, but many a rough hand must knead clay, and many an elbow be crooked to the stitch, to keep that body of yours warm and fine. Now remember, whatever you and your work may be worth, the less your keep costs, the better. It does not cost money only. It costs degradation. You do not merely employ these people. You also tread upon them. It cannot be helped;—you have your place, and they have theirs; but see that you tread as lightly as possible, and on as few as possible. What food, and clothes, and lodging, you honestly need, for your health and peace, you may righteously take. See that you take the plainest you can serve yourself with—that you waste or wear nothing vainly—and that you employ no man in furnishing you with any useless luxury."

130. That is the first lesson of Christian—

or human—economy; and depend upon it, my friend, it is a sound one, and has every voice and vote of the spirits of Heaven and earth to back it, whatever views the Manchester men, or any other manner of men, may take respecting "demand and supply." Demand what you deserve, and you shall be supplied with it, for your good. Demand what you do *not* deserve, and you shall be supplied with something which you have not demanded, and which Nature perceives that you deserve, quite to the contrary of your good. That is the law of your existence, and if you do not make it the law of your resolved acts, so much, precisely, the worse for you and all connected with you.

131. Yet observe, though it is out of its proper place said here, this law forbids no luxury which men are not degraded in providing. You may have Paul Veronese to paint your ceiling, if you like, or Benvenuto Cellini to make cups for you. But you must not employ a hundred divers to find beads to stitch over your sleeve. (Did you see the account of the sales of the Esterhazy jewels the other day?)

And the degree in which you recognise the difference between these two kinds of services, is precisely what makes the difference between your being a civilised person or a barbarian. If you keep slaves to furnish forth your dress—to glut your stomach—sustain your indolence—or deck your pride, you are a barbarian. If you keep servants, properly cared for, to furnish you with what you verily want, and no more than that—you are a "civil" person—a person capable of the qualities of citizenship.*

132. Now, farther, observe that in a truly civilised and disciplined state, no man would be allowed to meddle with any material who did not know how to make the best of it. In other words, the arts of working in wood, clay, stone, and metal, would all be *fine* arts (working in iron for machinery becoming an entirely distinct business). There would be no joiner's work, no smith's, no pottery nor stone-cutting, so debased in character as to be entirely unconnected with the finer branches of the same art; and to at least one of these finer branches (generally in metal-work) every painter and sculptor would be necessarily apprenticed during some years of his education. There would be room, in these four trades alone, for nearly

---

* Compare 'The Crown of Wild Olive.' §§ 79, 118, and 122

every grade of practical intelligence and productive imagination.

133. But it should not be artists alone who are exercised early in these crafts. It would be part of my scheme of physical education that every youth in the state—from the King's son downwards,—should learn to do something finely and thoroughly with his hand, so as to let him know what *touch* meant; and what stout craftsmanship meant; and to inform him of many things besides, which no man can learn but by some severely accurate discipline in doing. Let him once learn to take a straight shaving off a plank, or draw a fine curve without faltering, or lay a brick level in its mortar; and he has learned a multitude of other matters which no lips of man could ever teach him. He might choose his craft, but whatever it was, he should learn it to some sufficient degree of true dexterity: and the result would be, in after life, that among the middle classes a good deal of their house furniture would be made, and a good deal of rough work, more or less clumsily, but not ineffectively, got through, by the master himself and his sons, with much furtherance of their general health and peace of mind, and

increase of innocent domestic pride and pleasure, and to the extinction of a great deal of vulgar upholstery and other mean handicraft.

134. Farther. A great deal of the vulgarity, and nearly all the vice, of retail commerce, involving the degradation of persons occupied in it, depends simply on the fact that their minds are always occupied by the vital (or rather mortal) question of profits. I should at once put an end to this source of baseness by making all retail dealers merely salaried officers in the employ of the trade guilds; the stewards, that is to say, of the saleable properties of those guilds, and purveyors of such and such articles to a given number of families. A perfectly well-educated person might, without the least degradation, hold such an office as this, however poorly paid; and it would be precisely the fact of his being well educated which would enable him to fulfil his duties to the public without the stimulus of direct profit. Of course the current objection to such a system would be that no man, for a regularly paid salary, would take pains to please his customers; and the answer to that objection is, that if you can train a man to so much unselfishness as to

offer himself fearlessly to the chance of being shot, in the course of his daily duty, you can most assuredly, if you make it also a point of honour with him, train him to the amount of self-denial involved in looking you out with care such a piece of cheese or bacon as you have asked for.

135. You see that I have already much diminished the number of employments involving degradation; and raised the character of many of those that are left. There remain to be considered the necessarily painful or mechanical works of mining, forging, and the like: the unclean, noisome, or paltry manufactures —the various kinds of transport—(by merchant shipping, etc.) and the conditions of menial service.

It will facilitate the examination of these if we put them for the moment aside, and pass to the other division of our dilemma, the question, namely, what kind of lives our gentlemen and ladies are to live, for whom all this hard work is to be done.

LETTER XXII.

Of the Normal Position and Duties of the Upper Classes. General Statement of the Land Question.

April 17, 1867.

136. IN passing now to the statement of conditions affecting the interests of the upper classes, I would rather have addressed these closing letters to one of themselves than to you, for it is with their own faults and needs that each class is primarily concerned. As, however, unless I kept the letters private, this change of their address would be but a matter of courtesy and form, not of any true prudential use; and as besides I am now no more inclined to reticence—prudent or otherwise; but desire only to state the facts of our national economy as clearly and completely as may be, I pursue the subject without respect of persons.

137. Before examining what the occupation and estate of the upper classes ought, as far as

may reasonably be conjectured, finally to become, it will be well to set down in brief terms what they actually have been in past ages: for this, in many respects, they must also always be. The upper classes, broadly speaking, are originally composed of the best-bred (in the merely animal sense of the term), the most energetic, and most thoughtful, of the population, who either by strength of arm seize the land from the rest, and make slaves of them, or bring desert land into cultivation, over which they have therefore, within certain limits, true personal right; or, by industry, accumulate other property, or by choice devote themselves to intellectual pursuits, and, though poor, obtain an acknowledged superiority of position, shown by benefits conferred in discovery, or in teaching, or in gifts of art. This is all in the simple course of the law of nature; and the proper offices of the upper classes, thus distinguished from the rest, become, therefore, in the main threefold:—

138. (A) Those who are strongest of arm have for their proper function the restraint and punishment of vice, and the general maintenance of law and order; releasing only from its

original subjection to their power that which truly deserves to be emancipated.

(B) Those who are superior by forethought and industry, have for their function to be the providences of the foolish, the weak, and the idle; and to establish such systems of trade and distribution of goods as shall preserve the lower orders from perishing by famine, or any other consequence of their carelessness or folly, and to bring them all, according to each man's capacity, at last into some harmonious industry.

(C) The third class, of scholars and artists, of course, have for function the teaching and delighting of the inferior multitude.

The office of the upper classes, then, as a body, is to keep order among their inferiors, and raise them always to the nearest level with themselves of which those inferiors are capable. So far as they are thus occupied, they are invariably loved and reverenced intensely by all beneath them, and reach, themselves, the highest types of human power and beauty.

139. This, then, being the natural ordinance and function of aristocracy, its corruption, like that of all other beautiful things under the Devil's touch, is a very fearful one. Its

corruption is, that those who ought to be the rulers and guides of the people, forsake their task of painful honourableness; seek their own pleasure and pre-eminence only; and use their power, subtlety, conceded influence, prestige of ancestry, and mechanical instrumentality of martial power, to make the lower orders toil for them, and feed and clothe them for nothing, and become in various ways their living property, goods, and chattels, even to the point of utter regardlessness of whatever misery these serfs may suffer through such insolent domination, or they themselves, their masters, commit of crime to enforce it.

140. And this is especially likely to be the case when means of various and tempting pleasure are put within the reach of the upper classes by advanced conditions of national commerce and knowledge: and it is *certain* to be the case as soon as position among those upper classes becomes any way purchaseable with money, instead of being the assured measure of some kind of worth, (either strength of hand, or true wisdom of conduct, or imaginative gift). It has been becoming more and more the condition of the aristocracy of Europe, ever since

the fifteenth century; and is gradually bringing about its ruin, and in that ruin, checked only by the power which here and there a good soldier or true statesman achieves over the putrid chaos of its vain policy, the ruin of all beneath it; which can be arrested only, either by the repentance of that old aristocracy, (hardly to be hoped,) or by the stern substitution of other aristocracy worthier than it.

141. Corrupt as it may be, it and its laws together, I would at this moment, if I could, fasten every one of its institutions down with bands of iron, and trust for all progress and help against its tyranny simply to the patience and strength of private conduct. And if I had to choose, I would tenfold rather see the tyranny of old Austria triumphant in the old and new worlds, and trust to the chance (or rather the distant certainty) of some day seeing a true Emperor born to its throne, than, with every privilege of thought and act, run the most distant risk of seeing the thoughts of the people of Germany and England become like the thoughts of the people of America.

My American friends, of whom one, Charles Eliot Norton, of Cambridge, is the dearest I have in the world, tell me I know nothing about America. It may be so, and they must do me the justice to observe that I, therefore, usually *say* nothing about America. But this much I have said, because the Americans, as a nation, set their trust in liberty and in equality, of which I detest the one, and deny the possibility of the other; and because, also, as a nation, they are wholly undesirous of Rest, and incapable of it; irreverent of themselves, both in the present and in the future; discontented with what they are, yet having no ideal of anything which they desire to become.*

142. But, however corrupted, the aristocracy of any nation may thus be always divided into three great classes. First, the landed proprietors and soldiers, essentially one political body (for the possession of land can only be maintained

---

* Some following passages in this letter, containing personal references which might, in permanence, have given pain or offence, are now omitted—the substance of them being also irrelevant to my main purpose. These few words about the American war, with which they concluded, are, I think, worth retaining:—"All methods of right government are to be communicated to foreign nations by perfectness of example and gentleness of patiently expanded power, not suddenly, nor at the bayonet's point. And

by military power); secondly, the moneyed men and leaders of commerce; thirdly, the professional men and masters in science, art, and literature.

And we were to consider the proper duties of all these, and the laws probably expedient respecting them. Whereupon, in the outset, we are at once brought face to face with the great land question.

143. Great as it may be, it is wholly subordinate to those we have hitherto been considering. The laws you make regarding methods of labour, or to secure the genuineness of the things produced by it, affect the entire moral state of the nation, and all possibility of human happiness for them. The mode of distribution of the land only affects their numbers. By this or that law respecting land you decide whether the

though it is the duty of every nation to interfere, at bayonet point, if they have the strength to do so, to save any oppressed multitude, or even individual, from manifest violence, it is wholly unlawful to interfere in such matter, except with sacredly pledged limitation of the objects to be accomplished in the oppressed person's favour, and with absolute refusal of all selfish advantage and *increase of territory or of political power* which might otherwise accrue from the victory."

nation shall consist of fifty or of a hundred millions. But by this or that law respecting work, you decide whether the given number of millions shall be rogues, or honest men;—shall be wretches, or happy men. And the question of numbers is wholly immaterial, compared with that of character; or rather, its own materialness depends on the prior determination of character. Make your nation consist of knaves, and, as Emerson said long ago, it is but the case of any other vermin—"the more, the worse." Or, to put the matter in narrower limits, it is a matter of no final concern to any parent whether he shall have two children, or four; but matter of quite final concern whether those he has, shall, or shall not, deserve to be hanged. The great difficulty in dealing with the land question at all arises from the false, though very natural, notion on the part of many reformers, and of large bodies of the poor, that the division of the land among the said poor would be an immediate and everlasting relief to them. An *immediate* relief it would be to the extent of a small annual sum (you may easily calculate how little, if you choose) to each of them; on the strength of which accession to their finances, they would multiply into as much extra personality as the extra pence would sustain, and at that point be checked by starvation, exactly as they are now.

144. Any other form of pillage would benefit them only in like manner; and, in reality, the difficult part of the question respecting numbers, is, not where they shall be arrested, but what shall be the method of their arrest.

An island of a certain size has standing room only for so many people; feeding ground for a great many fewer than could stand on it. Reach the limits of your feeding ground, and you must cease to multiply, must emigrate or starve. The modes in which the pressure is gradually brought to bear on the population depend on the justice of your laws; but the pressure itself must come at last, whatever the distribution of the land. And arithmeticians seem to me a little slow to remark the importance of the old child's puzzle about the nails in the horseshoe—when it is populations that are doubling themselves, instead of farthings.

145. The essential land question, then, is to be treated quite separately from that of the methods of restriction of population. The land

question is—At what point will you resolve to stop? It is separate matter of discussion how you are to stop at it.

And this essential land question—"At what point will you stop?"—is itself two-fold. You have to consider first, by what methods of land distribution you can maintain the greatest number of healthy persons; and secondly, whether, if, by any other mode of distribution and relative ethical laws, you can raise their character, while you diminish their numbers, such sacrifice should be made, and to what extent? I think it will be better, for clearness' sake, to end this letter with the putting of these two queries in their decisive form, and to reserve suggestions of answer for my next.

LETTER XXIII.

Of the Just Tenure of Lands : and the proper Functions of high Public Officers.

20th April, 1867.

146. I MUST repeat to you, once more, before I proceed, that I only enter on this part of our enquiry to complete the sequence of its system, and explain fully the bearing of former conclusions, and not for any immediately practicable good to be got out of the investigation. Whatever I have hitherto urged upon you, it is in the power of all men quietly to promote, and finally to secure, by the patient resolution of personal conduct; but no action could be taken in redistribution of land or in limitation of the incomes of the upper classes, without grave and prolonged civil disturbance.

Such disturbance, however, is only too likely to take place, if the existing theories of political economy are allowed credence much longer. In the writings of the vulgar economists, nothing more excites my indignation than the subterfuges by which they endeavour to accommodate their pseudo-science to the existing abuses of wealth, by disguising the true nature of rent. I will not waste time in exposing their fallacies, but will put the truth for you into as clear a shape as I can.

147. Rent, of whatever kind, is, briefly, the price continuously paid for the loan of the property of another person. It may be too little, or it may be just, or exorbitant, or altogether unjustifiable, according to circumstances. Exorbitant rents can only be exacted from ignorant or necessitous rent-payers: and it is one of the most necessary conditions of state economy that there should be clear laws to prevent such exaction.

148. I may interrupt myself for a moment to give you an instance of what I mean. The most wretched houses of the poor in London often pay ten or fifteen per cent. to the landlord; and I have known an instance of sanitary legislation being hindered, to the loss of many hundreds of lives, in order that the rents of a nobleman, derived from the necessities of the poor, might not be diminished. And it is a

curious thing to me to see Mr. J. S. Mill foaming at the mouth, and really afflicted conscientiously, because he supposes one man to have been unjustly hanged, while by his own failure, (I believe, *wilful* failure)* in stating clearly to the public one of the first elementary truths of the science he professes, he is aiding and abetting the commission of the cruellest possible form of murder on many thousands of persons yearly, for the sake simply of putting money into the pockets of the landlords. I felt this evil so strongly that I bought, in the worst part of London, one freehold and one leasehold property, consisting of houses inhabited by the lowest poor; in order to try what change in their comfort and habits I could effect by taking only a just rent, but that firmly. The houses of the leasehold pay me five per cent.; the families that used to have one room in them have now two; and are more orderly and hopeful besides; and there is a surplus still on the rents they pay after I have taken my five per cent., with which, if all goes well, they will eventually be able to buy twelve years of the lease from me. The freehold pays three per

* See § 156.

cent., with similar results in the comfort of the tenant. This is merely an example of what might be done by firm State action in such matters.

149. Next, of wholly unjustifiable rents. These are for things which are not, and which it is criminal to consider as, personal or exchangeable property. Bodies of men, land, water, and air, are the principal of these things.

Parenthetically, may I ask you to observe, that though a fearless defender of some forms of slavery, I am no defender of the slave *trade*. It is by a blundering confusion of ideas between *governing* men, and *trading in* men, and by consequent interference with the restraint, instead of only with the sale, that most of the great errors in action have been caused among the emancipation men. I am prepared, if the need be clear to my own mind, and if the power is in my hands, to throw men into prison, or any other captivity—to bind them or to beat them—and force them, for such periods as I may judge necessary, to any kind of irksome labour : and on occasion of desperate resistance, to hang or shoot them. But I will not *sell* them.

150. Bodies of men, or women, then (and much more, as I said before, their souls), must not be bought or sold. Neither must land, nor water, nor air, these being the necessary sustenance of men's bodies and souls.

Yet all these may, on certain terms, be bound, or secured in possession, to particular persons under certain conditions. For instance, it may be proper, at a certain time, to give a man permission to possess land, as you give him permission to marry; and farther, if he wishes it and works for it, to secure to him the land needful for his life; as you secure his wife to him; and make both utterly his own, without in the least admitting his right to buy other people's wives, or fields, or to sell his own.

151. And the right action of a State respecting its land is, indeed, to secure it in various portions to those of its citizens who deserve to be trusted with it, according to their respective desires and proved capacities; and after having so secured it to each, to exercise only such vigilance over his treatment of it as the State must give also to his treatment of his wife and servants; for the most part leaving him free, but interfering in cases of

gross mismanagement or abuse of power. And in the case of great old families, which always ought to be, and in some measure, however decadent, still truly are, the noblest monumental architecture of the kingdom, living temples of sacred tradition and hero's religion, so much land ought to be granted to them in perpetuity as may enable them to live thereon with all circumstances of state and outward nobleness; *but their income must in no wise be derived from the rents of it*, nor must they be occupied (even in the most distant or subordinately administered methods), in the exaction of rents. That is not noblemen's work. Their income must be fixed, and paid them by the State, as the King's is.

152. So far from their land being to them a source of income, it should be, on the whole, costly to them, great part of it being kept in conditions of natural grace, which return no rent but their loveliness; and the rest made, at whatever cost, exemplary in perfection of such agriculture as develops the happiest peasant life;* agriculture which, as I will show you hereafter, must reject the aid of all mechanism

* Compare 'Fors Clavigera,' Letter XXI., page 22.

except that of instruments guided solely by the human hand, or by animal, or directly natural forces; and which, therefore, cannot compete for profitableness with agriculture carried on by aid of machinery.

And now for the occupation of this body of men, maintained at fixed perennial cost of the State.

153. You know I said I should want no soldiers of special skill or pugnacity, for all my boys would be soldiers. But I assuredly want *captains* of soldiers, of special skill and pugnacity. And also, I said I should strongly object to the appearance of any lawyers in my territory; meaning, however, by lawyers, people who live by arguing about law,—not people appointed to administer law; and people who live by eloquently misrepresenting facts,—not people appointed to discover and plainly represent them.

Therefore, the youth of this landed aristocracy would be trained, in my schools, to these two great callings, not *by* which, but *in* which, they are to live.

They would be trained, all of them, in perfect science of war, and in perfect science of essential law. And from their body should be chosen the captains and the judges of England, its advocates, and generally its State officers, all such functions being held for fixed pay (as already our officers of the Church and army are paid), and no function connected with the administration of law ever paid by casual fee. And the head of such family should, in his own right, having passed due (and high) examination in the science of law, and not otherwise, be a judge, law-ward or Lord, having jurisdiction both in civil and criminal cases, such as our present judges have, after such case shall have been fully represented before, and received verdict from, a jury, composed exclusively of the middle or lower orders, and in which no member of the aristocracy should sit. But from the decision of these juries, or from the Lord's sentence, there should be a final appeal to a tribunal, the highest in the land, held solely in the King's name, and over which, in the capital, the King himself should preside, and therein give judgment on a fixed number of days in each year;—and, in other places and at other times, judges appointed by election (under certain conditions) out of any order of men in the State (the election being national, not provincial): and all causes brought before these judges should be decided, without appeal, by their own authority; not by juries. This, then, recasting it for you into brief view, would be the entire scheme of state authorities:—

154. (1) The King: exercising, as part both of his prerogative and his duty, the office of a supreme judge at stated times in the central court of appeal of his kingdom.

(2) Supreme judges appointed by national election; exercising sole authority in courts of final appeal.

(3) Ordinary judges, holding the office hereditarily under conditions; and with power to add to their number (and liable to have it increased if necessary by the King's appointment); the office of such judges being to administer the national laws under the decision of juries.

(4) State officers charged with the direction of public agency in matters of public utility.

(5) Bishops, charged with offices of supervision and aid, to family by family, and person by person.

(6) The officers of war, of various ranks.

(7) The officers of public instruction, of various ranks.

I have sketched out this scheme for you somewhat prematurely, for I would rather have conducted you to it step by step, and as I brought forward the reasons for the several parts of it; but it is, on other grounds, desirable that you should have it to refer to, as I go on.

155. Without depending anywise upon nomenclature, yet holding it important as a sign and record of the meanings of things, I may tell you further that I should call the elected supreme judges, "Princes"; the hereditary judges, "Lords"; and the officers of public guidance, "Dukes"; and that the social rank of these persons would be very closely correspondent to that implied by such titles under our present constitution; only much more real and useful. And in conclusion of this letter, I will but add, that if you, or other readers, think it idle of me to write or dream of such things; as if any of them were in our power, or within possibility of any near realization, and above all, vain to write of them to a workman at Sunderland: you are to remember what I told

you at the beginning, that I go on with this part of my subject in some fulfilment of my long-conceived plan, too large to receive at present any deliberate execution from my failing strength; (being the body of the work to which 'Munera Pulveris' was intended merely as an introduction;) and that I address it to you because I know that the working men of England must, for some time, be the only body to which we can look for resistance to the deadly influence of moneyed power.

I intend, however, to write to you at this moment one more letter, partly explanatory of minor details necessarily omitted in this, and chiefly of the proper office of the soldier; and then I must delay the completion of even this poor task until after the days have turned, for I have quite other work to do in the brightness of the full-opened spring.

156. P.S.—As I have used somewhat strong language, both here and elsewhere, of the equivocations of the economists on the subject of rent, I had better refer you to one characteristic example. You will find in paragraph 5th and 6th of Book II., chap. 2, of Mr. Mill's 'Principles,' that the right to tenure of land is based,

by his admission, only on the proprietor's being its improver.

Without pausing to dwell on the objection that land cannot be improved beyond a certain point, and that, at the reaching of that point, farther claim to tenure would cease, on Mr. Mill's principle—take even this admission, with its proper subsequent conclusion, that "in no sound theory of private property was it ever contemplated that the proprietor of land should be merely a sinecurist quartered on it." Now, had that conclusion been farther followed, it would have compelled the admission that all rent was unjustifiable which normally maintained any person in idleness; which is indeed the whole truth of the matter. But Mr. Mill instantly retreats from this perilous admission; and after three or four pages of discussion (quite accurate for *its* part) of the limits of power in management of the land itself (which apply just as strictly to the peasant proprietor as to the cottier's landlord), he begs the whole question at issue in one brief sentence, slipped cunningly into the middle of a long one which appears to be telling all the other way, and in which the fatal assertion (of the right to rent) nestles itself, as if it had been already proved,—thus—I italicise the unproved assertion in which the venom of the entire falsehood is concentrated.

"Even in the case of cultivated land, a man whom, though only one among millions, the law permits to hold thousands of acres as his single share, is not entitled to think that all is given to him to use and abuse, and deal with it as if it concerned nobody but himself. *The rents or profits which he can obtain from it are his, and his only;* but with regard to the land, in everything which he abstains from doing, he is morally bound, and should, whenever the case admits, be legally compelled to make his interest and pleasure consistent with the public good."

157. I say, this sentence in italics is slipped *cunningly* into the long sentence, as if it were of no great consequence; and above I have expressed my belief that Mr. Mill's equivocations on this subject are wilful. It is a grave accusation; but I cannot, by any stretch of charity, attribute these misrepresentations to absolute dulness and bluntness of brain, either in Mr. Mill or his follower, Mr. Fawcett. Mr.

Mill is capable of immense involuntary error ; but his involuntary errors are usually owing to his seeing only one or two of the many sides of a thing; not to obscure sight of the side he *does* see. Thus his 'Essay on Liberty' only takes cognisance of facts that make for liberty, and of none that make for restraint. But in its statement of all that can be said for liberty, it is so clear and keen, that I have myself quoted it before now as the best authority on that side. And, if arguing in favour of Rent, absolutely, and with clear explanation of what it was, he had then defended it with all his might, I should have attributed to him only the honest shortsightedness of partisanship ; but when I find his defining sentences full of subtle entanglement and reserve—and that reserve held throughout his treatment of this particular subject,—I cannot, whether I utter the suspicion or not, keep the sense of wilfulness in the misrepresentation from remaining in my mind. And if there be indeed ground for this blame, and Mr. Mill, for fear of fostering political agitation,* *has* disguised what he knows to be

* With at last the natural consequences of cowardice,— nitro-glycerine and fire-balls ! Let the upper classes speak

the facts about rent, I would ask him as one of the leading members of the Jamaica Committee, which is the greater crime, boldly to sign warrant for the sudden death of one man, known to be an agitator, in the immediate outbreak of such agitation, or, by equivocation in a scientific work, to sign warrants for the deaths of thousands of men in slow misery, for *fear* of an agitation which has not begun; and if begun, would be carried on by debate, not by the sword?

the truth about themselves boldly, and they will know how to defend themselves fearlessly. It is equivocation in principle, and dereliction from duty, which melt at last into tears in a mob's presence.—(Dec. 16th, 1867.)

LETTER XXIV.

The Office of the Soldier.

April 22, 1867.

158. I MUST once more deprecate your probable supposition that I bring forward this ideal plan of State government, either with any idea of its appearing, to our present public mind, practicable even at a remote period, or with any positive and obstinate adherence to the particular form suggested. There are no wiser words among the many wise ones of the most rational and keen-sighted of old English men of the world, than these:—

> " For forms of government let fools contest;
> That which is best administered is best."

For, indeed, no form of government is of any use among bad men; and any form will work in the hands of the good; but the essence of all government among good men is this, that it is mainly occupied in the *production and recognition of human worth,* and in the detection and extinction of human unworthiness; and every Government which produces and recognises worth, will also inevitably use the worth it has found to govern with; and therefore fall into some approximation to such a system as I have described. And, as I told you, I do not contend for names, nor particular powers—though I state those which seem to me most advisable; on the contrary, I know that the precise extent of authorities must be different in every nation at different times, and ought to be so, according to their circumstances and character; and all that I assert with confidence is the necessity, within afterwards definable limits, of *some such* authorities as these; that is to say,

159. I. An *observant* one :—by which all men shall be looked after and taken note of.

II. A *helpful* one, from which those who need help may get it.

III. A *prudential* one, which shall not let people dig in wrong places for coal, nor make railroads where they are not wanted; and which shall also, with true providence, insist on their digging in right places for coal, in a safe manner, and making railroads where they *are* wanted.

IV. A *martial* one, which will punish knaves and make idle persons work.

V. An *instructive* one, which shall tell everybody what it is their duty to know, and be ready pleasantly to answer questions if anybody asks them.

VI. A *deliberate* and *decisive* one, which shall judge by law, and amend or make law;

VII. An *exemplary* one, which shall show what is loveliest in the art of life.

You may divide or name those several offices as you will, or they may be divided in practice as expediency may recommend; the plan I have stated merely puts them all into the simplest forms and relations.

160. You see I have just defined the martial power as that "which punishes knaves and makes idle persons work." For that is indeed the ultimate and perennial soldiership; that is the essential warrior's office to the end of time. "There is no discharge in that war." To the compelling of sloth, and the scourging of sin, the strong hand will have to address itself as long as this wretched little dusty and volcanic world breeds nettles, and spits fire. The soldier's office at present is indeed supposed to be the defence of his country against other countries; but that is an office which—Utopian as

you may think the saying—will soon now be extinct. I say so fearlessly, though I say it with wide war threatened, at this moment, in the East and West. For observe what the standing of nations on their defence really means. It means that, but for such armed attitude, each of them would go and rob the other; that is to say, that the majority of active persons in every nation are at present—thieves. I am very sorry that this should still be so; but it will not be so long. National exhibitions, indeed, will not bring peace; but national education will, and that is soon coming. I can judge of this by my own mind, for I am myself naturally as covetous a person as lives in this world, and am as eagerly-minded to go and steal some things the French have got, as any housebreaker could be, having clue to attractive spoons. If I could by military incursion carry off Paul Veronese's "Marriage in Cana," and the "Venus Victrix," and the "Hours of St. Louis," it would give me the profoundest satisfaction to accomplish the foray successfully; nevertheless, being a comparatively educated person, I should most assuredly not give myself that satisfaction, though there were not an ounce of gunpowder, nor a bayonet, in all France. I have not the least mind to rob anybody, however much I may covet what they have got; and I know that the French and British public may and will, with many other publics, be at last brought to be of this mind also; and to see farther that a nation's real strength and happiness do not depend on properties and territories, nor on machinery for their defence; but on their getting such territory as they *have*, well filled with none but respectable persons. Which is a way of *infinitely* enlarging one's territory, feasible to every potentate; and dependent no wise on getting Trent turned, or Rhine-edge reached.

161. Not but that, in the present state of things, it may often be soldiers' duty to seize territory, and hold it strongly; but only from banditti, or savage and idle persons.

Thus, both Calabria and Greece ought to have been irresistibly occupied long ago. Instead of quarrelling with Austria about Venice, the Italians ought to have made a truce with her for ten years, on condition only of her destroying no monuments, and not taxing Italians more than Germans; and then thrown the whole force of their army on Calabria, shot down every bandit in it in a week, and forced the peasantry of it into honest work on every hill-side, with stout and immediate help from the soldiers in embanking streams, building walls, and the like; and Italian finance would have been a much pleasanter matter for the King to take account of by this time; and a fleet might have been floating under Garganus strong enough to sweep every hostile sail out of the Adriatic, instead of a disgraced and useless remnant of one, about to be put up to auction.

And similarly, *we* ought to have occupied Greece instantly, when they asked us, whether Russia liked it or not; given them an English king, made good roads for them, and stout laws; and kept them, and their hills and seas, with righteous shepherding of Arcadian fields, and righteous ruling of Salaminian wave, until they could have given themselves a Greek king of men again; and obeyed him, like men.

April 24.

162. It is strange that just before I finish work for this time, there comes the first real and notable sign of the victory of the principles I have been fighting for, these seven years. It

is only a newspaper paragraph, but it means much. Look at the second column of the 11th page of yesterday's 'Pall Mall Gazette.' The paper has taken a wonderful fit of misprinting lately (unless my friend John Simon has been knighted on his way to Weimar, which would be much too right and good a thing to be a likely one); but its straws of talk mark which way the wind blows perhaps more early than those of any other journal—and look at the question it puts in that page, "Whether political economy be the sordid and materialistic science some account it, or almost the noblest on which thought can be employed?" Might not you as well have determined that question a little while ago, friend Public? and known what political economy *was*, before you talked so much about it?

But, hark, again — " Ostentation, parental pride, and a host of moral" (immoral?) "qualities must be recognised as among the springs of industry; political economy should not ignore these, but, to discuss them, *it must abandon its pretensions to the precision of a pure science.*"

163. Well done the 'Pall Mall'! Had it written " Prudence and parental affection," instead

of "Ostentation and parental pride," "must be recognised among the springs of industry," it would have been still better; and it would then have achieved the expression of a part of the truth, which I put into clear terms in the first sentence of 'Unto this Last,' in the year 1862 —which it has thus taken five years to get half way into the public's head.

"Among the delusions which at different periods have possessed themselves of the minds of large masses of the human race, perhaps the most curious—certainly the least creditable —is the modern *soi-disant* science of political economy, based on the idea that an advantageous code of social action may be determined, irrespectively of the influence of social affection."

Look also at the definition of skill, p. 87.

"Under the term 'skill' I mean to include the united force of experience, intellect, and passion, in their operation on manual labour, and under the term 'passion' to include the entire range of the moral feelings."

164. I say half way into the public's head, because you see, a few lines further on, the 'Pall Mall' hopes for a pause "half way between

the rigidity of Ricardo and the sentimentality of Ruskin."

With one hand on their pocket, and the other on their heart! Be it so for the present; we shall see how long this statuesque attitude can be maintained; meantime, it chances strangely —as several other things have chanced while I was writing these notes to you—that they should have put in that sneer (two lines before) at my note on the meaning of the Homeric and Platonic Sirens, at the very moment when I was doubting whether I would or would not tell you the significance of the last song of Ariel in 'The Tempest.'

I had half determined not, but now I shall. And this was what brought me to think of it:—

165. Yesterday afternoon I called on Mr. H. C. Sorby, to see some of the results of an inquiry he has been following all last year, into the nature of the colouring matter of leaves and flowers.

You most probably have heard (at all events, may with little trouble hear) of the marvellous power which chemical analysis has received in recent discoveries respecting the laws of light.

My friend showed me the rainbow of the

rose, and the rainbow of the violet, and the rainbow of the hyacinth, and the rainbow of forest leaves being born, and the rainbow of forest leaves dying.

And, last, he showed me the rainbow of blood. It was but the three-hundredth part of a grain, dissolved in a drop of water; and it cast its measured bars, for ever recognisable now to human sight, on the chord of the seven colours. And no drop of that red rain can now be shed, so small as that the stain of it cannot be known, and the voice of it heard out of the ground.

166. But the seeing these flower colours, and the iris of blood together with them, just while I was trying to gather into brief space the right laws of war, brought vividly back to me my dreaming fancy of long ago, that even the trees of the earth were "capable of a kind of sorrow, as they opened their innocent leaves in vain for men; and along the dells of England her beeches cast their dappled shades only where the outlaw drew his bow, and the king rode his careless chase; amidst the fair defiles of the Apennines, the twisted olive-trunks hid the ambushes of treachery, and on their meadows,

day by day, the lilies, which were white at the dawn, were washed with crimson at sunset."

And so also now this chance word of the daily journal, about the Sirens, brought to my mind the divine passage in the Cratylus of Plato, about the place of the dead.

"And none of those who dwell there desire to depart thence,—no, not even the Sirens; but even they, the seducers, are there themselves beguiled, and they who lulled all men, themselves laid to rest—they, and all others—such sweet songs doth death know how to sing to them."

So also the Hebrew.

"And desire shall fail, because man goeth to his long home." For you know I told you the Sirens were not pleasures, but desires; being always represented in old Greek art as having human faces, with birds' wings and feet; and sometimes with eyes upon their wings; and there are not two more important passages in all literature, respecting the laws of labour and of life, than those two great descriptions of the Sirens in Homer and Plato,—the Sirens of death, and Sirens of eternal life, representing severally the earthly and heavenly desires of men; the heavenly desires singing to the motion of circles of the spheres, and the earthly on the rocks of fatallest shipwreck. A fact which may indeed be regarded "sentimentally," but it is also a profoundly important politico-economical one.

And now for Shakspeare's song.

167. You will find, if you look back to the analysis of it, given in 'Munera Pulveris,' § 134, that the whole play of 'The Tempest' is an allegorical representation of the powers of true, and therefore spiritual, Liberty, as opposed to true, and therefore carnal and brutal Slavery. There is not a sentence nor a rhyme, sung or uttered by Ariel or Caliban, throughout the play, which has not this under-meaning.

168. Now the fulfilment of all human liberty is in the peaceful inheritance of the earth, with its "herb yielding seed, and fruit tree yielding fruit" after his kind; the pasture, or arable, land, and the blossoming, or wooded and fruited, land uniting the final elements of life and peace, for body and soul. Therefore, we have the two great Hebrew forms of benediction, "His eyes shall be red with wine, and his teeth white with milk," and again, "Butter and honey shall he eat, that he may know to refuse the evil and

choose the good." And as the work of war and sin has always been the devastation of this blossoming earth, whether by spoil or idleness, so the work of peace and virtue is also that of the first day of Paradise, to "Dress it and to keep it." And that will always be the song of perfectly accomplished Liberty, in her industry, and rest, and shelter from troubled thoughts in the calm of the fields, and gaining, by migration, the long summer's day from the shortening twilight:—

> "Where the bee sucks, there lurk I;
> In a cowslip's bell I lie;
> There I couch when owls do cry.
> On the bat's back I do fly
> After summer merrily:
> Merrily, merrily, shall I live now
> Under the blossom that hangs on the bough."

And the security of this treasure to all the poor, and not the ravage of it down the valleys of the Shenandoah, is indeed the true warrior's work. But, that they may be able to restrain vice rightly, soldiers must themselves be first in virtue; and that they may be able to compel labour sternly, they must themselves be first in toil, and their spears, like Jonathan's at Bethaven, enlighteners of the eyes.

LETTER XXV.

Of inevitable Distinction of Rank, and necessary Submission to authority. The meaning of Pure-Heartedness. Conclusion.

169. I WAS interrupted yesterday, just as I was going to set my soldiers to work; and to-day, here comes the pamphlet you promised me, containing the Debates about Church-going, in which I find so interesting a text for my concluding letter that I must still let my soldiers stand at ease for a little while. Look at its twenty-fifth page, and you will find, in the speech of Mr. Thomas, (carpenter,) this beautiful explanation of the admitted change in the general public mind, of which Mr. Thomas, for his part, highly approves, (the getting out of the unreasonable habit of paying respect to anybody.) There were many reasons to Mr. Thomas's mind why the working classes did not attend places of worship: one was, that "the parson was regarded as an object of reverence. In the little town he came from, if a

poor man did not make a bow to the parson he was a marked man. This was no doubt wearing away to a great extent" (the base habit of making bows), "because, the poor man was beginning to get education, and to think for himself. It was only while the priest kept the press from him that he was kept ignorant, and was compelled to bow, as it were, to the parson. . . . It was the case all over England. The clergyman seemed to think himself something superior. Now he (Mr. Thomas) did not admit there was any inferiority" (laughter, audience throughout course of meeting mainly in the right), "except, perhaps, on the score of his having received a classical education, which the poor man could not get."

Now, my dear friend, here is the element which is the veriest devil of all that have got into modern flesh; this infidelity of the nineteenth century St. Thomas in there being anything better than himself alive; * coupled, as it always is, with the farther resolution—if unwillingly convinced of the fact,—to seal the Better living thing down again out of his way, under the first stone handy. I had not intended,

* Compare 'Crown of Wild Olive,' § 136.

till we entered on the second section of our enquiry, namely, into the influence of gentleness (having hitherto, you see, been wholly concerned with that of justice), to give you the clue out of our dilemma about equalities produced by education; but by the speech of our superior carpenter, I am driven into it at once, and it is perhaps as well.

170. The speech is not, observe, without its own root of truth at the bottom of it, nor at all, as I think, ill intended by the speaker; but you have in it a clear instance of what I was saying in the sixteenth of these letters,—that education *was desired by the lower orders because they thought it would make them upper orders*, and be a leveller and effacer of distinctions. They will be mightily astonished, when they really get it, to find that it is, on the contrary, the fatallest of all discerners and enforcers of distinctions; piercing, even to the division of the joints and marrow, to find out wherein your body and soul are less, or greater, than other bodies and souls, and to sign deed of separation with unequivocal seal.

171. Education is, indeed, of all differences not divinely appointed, an instant effacer and

reconciler. Whatever is undivinely poor, it will make rich; whatever is undivinely maimed, and halt, and blind, it will make whole, and equal, and seeing. The blind and the lame are to it as to David at the siege of the Tower of the Kings, "hated of David's soul." But there are other divinely-appointed differences, eternal as the ranks of the everlasting hills, and as the strength of their ceaseless waters. And these, education does *not* do away with; but measures, manifests, and employs.

In the handful of shingle which you gather from the sea-beach, which the indiscriminate sea, with equality of fraternal foam, has only educated to be, every one, round, you will see little difference between the noble and mean stones. But the jeweller's trenchant education of them will tell you another story. Even the meanest will be better for it, but the noblest so much better that you can class the two together no more. The fair veins and colours are all clear now, and so stern is nature's intent regarding this, that not only will the polish show which is best, but the best will take most polish. You shall not merely see they have more virtue than the others, but see that more of virtue more clearly; and the less virtue there is, the more dimly you shall see what there is of it.

172. And the law about education, which is sorrowfullest to vulgar pride, is this—that all its gains are at compound interest; so that, as our work proceeds, every hour throws us farther behind the greater men with whom we began on equal terms. Two children go to school hand in hand, and spell for half an hour over the same page. Through all their lives, never shall they spell from the same page more. One is presently a page a-head,—two pages, ten pages,—and evermore, though each toils equally, the interval enlarges—at birth nothing, at death, infinite.

173. And by this you may recognise true education from false. False education is a delightful thing, and warms you, and makes you every day think more of yourself. And true education is a deadly cold thing, with a Gorgon's head on her shield, and makes you every day think worse of yourself.

Worse in two ways, also, more's the pity. It is perpetually increasing the personal sense of ignorance and the personal sense of fault. And this last is the truth which is at the bottom of the common evangelical notion about conversion, and which the Devil has got hold of, and hidden, until, instead of seeing and confessing personal ignorance and fault, as compared with the sense and virtue of others, people see nothing but corruption in human nature, and shelter their own sins under accusation of their race (the worst of all assertions of equality and fraternity). And so they avoid the blessed and strengthening pain of finding out wherein they are fools, as compared with other men, by calling everybody else a fool too; and avoid the pain of discerning their own faults, by vociferously claiming their share in the great capital of original sin.

I must also, therefore, tell you here what properly ought to have begun the next following section of our subject—the point usually unnoticed in the parable of the Prodigal Son.

174. First, have you ever observed that all Christ's main teachings, by direct order, by earnest parable, and by His own permanent emotion, regard the use and misuse of *money*? We might have thought, if we had been asked what a divine teacher was most likely to teach, that he would have left inferior persons to give directions about money; and himself spoken

only concerning faith and love, and the discipline of the passions, and the guilt of the crimes of soul against soul. But not so. He speaks in general terms of these. But He does not speak parables about them for all men's memory, nor permit Himself fierce indignation against them, in all men's sight. The Pharisees bring Him an adulteress. He writes her forgiveness on the dust of which He had formed her. Another, despised of all for known sin, He recognised as a giver of unknown love. But He acknowledges no love in buyers and sellers in His house. One should have thought there were people in that house twenty times worse than they;—Caiaphas and his like—false priests, false prayer-makers, false leaders of the people—who needed putting to silence, or to flight, with darkest wrath. But the scourge is only against the *traffickers and thieves*. The two most intense of all the parables: the two which lead the rest in love and terror (this of the Prodigal, and of Dives), relate, both of them, to management of riches. The practical order given to the only seeker of advice, of whom it is recorded that Christ "loved him," is briefly about his property. "Sell that thou hast."

And the arbitrament of the day of the Last Judgment is made to rest wholly, neither on belief in God, nor in any spiritual virtue in man, nor on freedom from stress of stormy crime, but on this only, "I was an hungered and ye gave me drink; naked, and ye clothed me; sick, and ye came unto me."

175. Well, then, the first thing I want you to notice in the parable of the Prodigal Son (and the last thing which people usually *do* notice in it), is—that it is about a Prodigal! He begins by asking for his share of his father's goods; he gets it, carries it off, and wastes it. It is true that he wastes it in riotous living, but you are not asked to notice in what kind of riot: he spends it with harlots—but it is not the harlotry which his elder brother accuses him of mainly, but of having devoured his father's living. Nay, it is not the sensual life which he accuses himself of—or which the manner of his punishment accuses him of. But the *wasteful* life. It is not said that he hadbecome debauched in soul, or diseased in body, by his vice; but that at last he would fain have filled his belly with husks, and could not. It is not said that he was struck with remorse for the consequences of his evil

passions, but only that he remembered there was bread enough and to spare, even for the servants, at home.

Now, my friend, do not think I want to extenuate sins of passion (though, in very truth, the sin of Magdalene is a light one compared to that of Judas); but observe, sins of passion, if of *real* passion, are often the errors and backfalls of noble souls; but prodigality is mere and pure selfishness, and essentially the sin of an ignoble or undeveloped creature; and I would rather, ten times rather, hear of a youth that (certain degrees of temptation and conditions of resistance being understood) he had fallen into any sin you chose to name, of all the mortal ones, than that he was in the habit of running bills which he could not pay.

Farther, though I hold that the two crowning and most accursed sins of the society of this present day are the carelessness with which it regards the betrayal of women, and the brutality with which it suffers the neglect of children, both these head and chief crimes, and all others, are rooted first in abuse of the laws, and neglect of the duties concerning wealth. And thus the love of money, with the parallel (and, observe, *mathematically commensurate* looseness in management of it), the "mal tener," followed necessarily by the "mal dare," is, indeed, the root of all evil.

176. Then, secondly, I want you to note that when the prodigal comes to his senses, he complains of nobody but himself, and speaks of no unworthiness but his own. He says nothing against any of the women who tempted him—nothing against the citizen who left him to feed on husks—nothing of the false friends of whom "no man gave unto him"—above all, nothing of the "corruption of human nature," or the corruption of things in general. He says that *he himself* is unworthy, as distinguished from honourable persons, and that *he himself* has sinned, as distinguished from righteous persons. And *that* is the hard lesson to learn, and the beginning of faithful lessons. All right and fruitful humility, and purging of heart, and seeing of God, is in that. It is easy to call yourself the chief of sinners, expecting every sinner round you to decline—or return—the compliment; but learn to measure the real degrees of your own relative baseness, and to be ashamed, not in heaven's sight, but in man's sight; and

redemption is indeed begun. Observe the phrase, I have sinned "*against* heaven," against the great law of that, and *before* thee, visibly degraded before my human sire and guide, unworthy any more of being esteemed of his blood, and desirous only of taking the place I deserve among his servants.

177. Now, I do not doubt but that I shall set many a reader's teeth on edge by what he will think my carnal and material rendering of this "beautiful" parable. But I am just as ready to spiritualise it as he is, provided I am sure first that we understand it. If we want to understand the parable of the sower, we must first think of it as of literal husbandry; if we want to understand the parable of the prodigal, we must first understand it as of literal prodigality. And the story has also for us a precious lesson in this literal sense of it, namely this, which I have been urging upon you throughout these letters, that all redemption must begin in subjection, and in the recovery of the sense of Fatherhood and authority, as all ruin and desolation begin in the loss of that sense. The lost son began by claiming his rights. He is found when he resigns them. He is lost by

flying from his father, when his father's authority was only paternal. He is found by returning to his father, and desiring that his authority may be absolute, as over a hired stranger.

And this is the practical lesson I want to leave with you, and all other working men.

178. You are on the eve of a great political crisis; and every rascal with a tongue in his head will try to make his own stock out of you. Now this is the test you must try them with. Those that say to you, "Stand up for your rights—get your division of living—be sure that you are as well off as others, and have what they have!—don't let any man dictate to you— have not you all a right to your opinion?—are you not all as good as everybody else?—let us have no governors, or fathers—let us all be free and alike." Those, I say, who speak thus to you, take Nelson's rough order for—and hate them as you do the Devil, for they *are* his ambassadors. But those, the few, who have the courage to say to you, "My friends, you and I, and all of us, have somehow got very wrong; we've been hardly treated, certainly; but here we are in a piggery, mainly by our own fault, hungry enough, and for ourselves, anything but

respectable: we *must* get out of this; there are certainly laws we may learn to live by, and there are wiser people than we are in the world, and kindly ones, if we can find our way to them; and an infinitely wise and kind Father, above all of them and us, if we can but find our way to *Him*, and ask Him to take us for servants, and put us to any work He will, so that we may never leave Him more." The people who will say that to you, and (for by *no* saying, but by their fruits, only, you shall finally know them) who are themselves orderly and kindly, and do their own business well,—take *those* for your guides, and trust them; on ice and rock alike, tie yourselves well together with them, and with much scrutiny, and cautious walking (perhaps nearly as much back as forward, at first), you will verily get off the glacier, and into meadow land, in God's time.

179. I meant to have written much to you respecting the meaning of that word "hired servants," and to have gone on to the duties of soldiers, for you know "Soldier" means a person who is paid to fight with regular pay—literally with "soldi" or "sous"—the "penny a day" of the vineyard labourers: but I can't now: only

just this much, that our whole system of work must be based on the nobleness of soldiership—so that we shall all be soldiers of either ploughshare or sword; and literally all our actual and professed soldiers, whether professed for a time only, or for life, must be kept to hard work of hand, when not in actual war; their honour consisting in being set to service of more pain and danger than others; to life-boat service; to redeeming of ground from furious rivers or sea—or mountain ruin; to subduing wild and unhealthy land, and extending the confines of colonies in the front of miasm and famine, and savage races.

And much of our harder home work must be done in a kind of soldiership, by bands of trained workers sent from place to place and town to town; doing, with strong and sudden hand, what is needed for help, and setting all things in more prosperous courses for the future.

Of all which I hope to speak in its proper place after we know what offices the higher arts of gentleness have among the lower ones of force, and how their prevalence may gradually change spear to pruning-hook, over the face of all the earth.

180. And now—but one word more—either

for you, or any other readers who may be startled at what I have been saying, as to the peculiar stress laid by the Founder of our religion on right dealing with wealth. Let them be assured that it is with no fortuitous choice among the attributes or powers of evil, that "Mammon" is assigned for the direct adversary of the Master whom they are bound to serve. You cannot, by any artifice of reconciliation, be God's soldier, and his. Nor while the desire of gain is within your heart, can any true knowledge of the Kingdom of God come there. No one shall enter its stronghold,—no one receive its blessing, except, "he that hath clean hands and a pure heart;" clean hands that have done no cruel deed,—pure heart, that knows no base desire. And, therefore, in the highest spiritual sense that can be given to words, be assured, not respecting the literal temple of stone and gold, but of the living temple of your body and soul, that no redemption, nor teaching, nor hallowing, will be anywise possible for it, until these two verses have been, for it also, fulfilled:—

"And He went into the temple, and began to cast out them that sold therein, and them that bought. And He taught daily in the temple."

APPENDICES.

———◆———

APPENDIX I.

Page 21.—*Expenditure on Science and Art.*

THE following is the passage referred to. The fact it relates is so curious, and so illustrative of our national interest in science, that I do not apologise for the repetition :—

"Two years ago there was a collection of the fossils of Solenhofen to be sold in Bavaria; the best in existence, containing many specimens unique for perfectness, and one, unique as an example of a species (a whole kingdom of unknown living creatures being announced by that fossil). This collection, of which the mere market worth, among private buyers, would probably have been some thousand or twelve hundred pounds, was offered to the English nation for seven hundred: but we would not give seven hundred, and the whole series would have been in the Munich museum at this moment, if Professor Owen* had not, with loss

---

* I originally stated this fact without Professor Owen's permission; which, of course, he could not with propriety

of his own time, and patient tormenting of the British public in the person of its representatives, got leave to give four hundred pounds at once, and himself become answerable for the other three!—which the said public will doubtless pay him eventually, but sulkily, and caring nothing about the matter all the while; only always ready to cackle if any credit comes of it. Consider, I beg of you, arithmetically, what this fact means. Your annual expenditure for public purposes (a third of it for military apparatus) is at least fifty millions. Now seven hundred pounds is to fifty million pounds, roughly, as seven pence to two thousand pounds. Suppose, then, a gentleman of unknown income, but whose wealth was to be conjectured from the fact that he spent two thousand a year on his park walls and footmen only, professes himself fond of science; and that one of his servants comes eagerly to tell him that an unique collection of fossils, giving clue to a new era of creation, is to be had for the sum of sevenpence sterling; and that the gentleman who is fond of science, and spends two thousand a year on his park, answers, after keeping his servant waiting several months, 'Well, I'll give you fourpence for them, if you will be answerable for the extra threepence yourself till next year.'"

have granted, had I asked it; but I considered it so important that the public should be aware of the fact, that I did what seemed to me right, though rude.

APPENDIX II.

Page 33.—*Legislation of Frederick the Great.*

THE following are the portions of Mr. Dixon's letters referred to :—

"Well, I am now busy with Frederick the Great; I am not now astonished that Carlyle calls him Great, neither that this work of his should have had such a sad effect upon him in producing it, when I see the number of volumes he must have had to wade through to produce such a clear terse set of utterances; and yet I do not feel the work as a book likely to do a reader of it the good that some of his other books will do. It is truly awful to read these battles after battles, lies after lies, called Diplomacy; it's fearful to read all this, and one wonders how he that set himself to this—He, of all men—could have the rare patience to produce such a laboured, heart-rending piece of work. Again, when one reads of the stupidity, the shameful waste of our moneys by our forefathers, to see our National Debt (the curse to our labour now, the millstone to our commerce, to our fair chance of competition in our day) thus created, and for what? Even Carlyle cannot tell; then how are we to tell? Now, who will deliver us? that is the question; who will help us in these days of *idle or no work*, while our foreign neighbours have plenty and are actually selling their produce to our men of capital cheaper than we can make it! House-rent getting dearer, taxes getting dearer, rates, clothing, food, etc. Sad times, my master, do seem to have fallen upon us. And the cause of nearly all this lies embedded in that Frederick; and yet, so far as I know of it, no critic has yet given an exposition of such laying there. For our behoof, is there no one that will take this, that there lies so woven in with much other stuff so sad to read, to any man that does not believe man was made to fight alone, to be a butcher of his fellow-man? Who will do this work, or piece of work, so that all who care may know how it is that our debt grew so large, and a great deal more that we ought to know?—that clearly is one great reason why the book was written and was printed. Well, I hope some day all this will be clear to our people, and some man or men will arise and sweep us clear of these hindrances, these sad drawbacks to the vitality of our work in this world."

"57, Nile Street, Sunderland, Feb. 7, 1867.

"Dear Sir,—

"I beg to acknowledge the receipt of two letters as additions to your books, which I have read with deep interest, and shall take care of them, and read them over again, so that I may thoroughly comprehend them, and be able to think of them for future use. I myself am not fully satisfied with our co-operation, and never have been; it is too much tinged with the very elements that they complain of in our present systems of trade—selfishness. I have for years been trying to direct the attention of the editor of the *Co-operator* to such evils that I see in it. Now further, I may state that I find you and Carlyle seem to agree quite on the idea of the *Masterhood* qualification. There again I find you both feel and write as all working men consider just. I can assure you there is not an honest, noble working man that would not by far serve under such *master*-hood, than be the employé or workman of a co-operative store. Working men do not as a rule make good masters; neither do they treat each other with that courtesy as a noble master treats his working man. George Fox shadows forth some such treatment that Friends ought to make law and guidance for their working men and slaves, such as you speak of in your letters. I will look the passage up; as it is quite to the point, so far as I now remember it. In Vol. VI. of *Frederick the Great*, I find a great deal there that I feel quite certain, if our Queen or Government could make law, thousands of English working men would hail it with such a shout of joy and gladness as would astonish the Continental world. These changes suggested by Carlyle and placed before the thinkers of England, are the noblest, the truest utterances on real kinghood, that I have ever read; the more I think over them, the more I feel the truth, the justness, and also the fitness of them, to our nation's present dire necessities; yet this is the man, and these are the thoughts of his, that our critics seem never to see, or if seen, don't think worth printing or in any way wisely directing the attention of the public thereto, alas! All this and much more fills me with such sadness that I am driven almost to despair. I see from the newspapers, Yorkshire, Lancashire, and other places are sternly endeavouring to carry out the short time movement until such times as trade revives, and I find the masters and men seem to adopt it with a good grace and friendly spirit. I also beg to inform you I see a Mr. Morley, a large manufacturer at Nottingham, has been giving pensions to all his old workmen. I hope such a noble example will be followed by other wealthy masters. It would do more to make a master loved, honoured, and cared for, than thousands of pounds expended in other ways. The Government Savings Banks is one of the wisest acts of late years done by our Government. I, myself, often wish the Government held all our banks instead of private men; that would put an end to false speculations, such as we too often in the provinces suffer so severely by, so I hail with pleasure and delight the shadowing forth by you of these noble plans for the future: I feel glad and uplifted to think of the good that such teaching will do for us all.

"Yours truly,
"Thomas Dixon."

APPENDICES.

"57, Nile Street, Sunderland, Feb. 24, 1867.

"DEAR SIR,—

"I now give you the references to *Frederick the Great.* Vol. VI.: Land Question, 365 page, where he increases the number of small farmers to 4,000 (202, 204). English soldiers and T. C.'s remarks on our system of purchase, etc. His law, (620, 623, 624.) State of Poland and how he repaired it, (487, 488, 489, 490). I especially value the way he introduced all kinds of industries therein, and so soon changed the chaos into order. Again, the schoolmasters also are given (not yet in England, says T. C.). Again the use he made of 15,000*l.* surplus in Brandenburg; how it was applied to better his staff of masters. To me, the Vol. VI. is one of the wisest pieces of modern thought in our language. I only wish I had either your power, C. Kingsley, Maurice, or some such able pen-generalship, to illustrate and show forth all the wise teaching on law, government, and social life I see in it, and shining like a star through all its pages.* I feel also the truth of all you have written, and will do all I can to make such men or women that care for such thoughts, see it, or read it. I am copying the letters as fast and as well as I can, and

---

* I have endeavoured to arrange some of the passages to which Mr. Dixon here refers, in a form enabling the reader to see their bearing on each other more distinctly, as a sequel to the essay on War in the 'Crown of Wild Olive.'

will use my utmost endeavour to have them done that justice to they merit.

"Yours truly,
"Thomas Dixon."

APPENDIX III.

Page 33.—*Effect of Modern Entertainments on the Mind of Youth.*

The letter of the *Times'* correspondent referred to contained an account of one of the most singular cases of depravity ever brought before a criminal court; but it is unnecessary to bring any of its details under the reader's attention, for nearly every other number of our journals has of late contained some instances of atrocities before unthought of, and, it might have seemed, impossible to humanity. The connection of these with the modern love of excitement in the sensational novel and drama may not be generally understood, but it is direct and constant; all furious pursuit of pleasure ending in actual desire of horror and delight in death. I entered into some fuller particulars on this subject in a lecture given in the spring at the Royal Institution.

[Any part of the lecture referred to likely to be of permanent interest will be printed, somewhere, in this series.]

APPENDIX IV.

Page 76.—*Drunkenness as the Cause of Crime.*

THE following portions of Mr. Dixon's letter referred to, will be found interesting :—

" DEAR SIR,—

"Your last letter, I think, will arouse the attention of thinkers more than any of the series, it being on topics they in general feel more interested in than the others, especially as in these you do not assail their pockets so much as in the former ones. Since you seem interested with the notes or rough sketches on gin, G * * * of Dublin was the man I alluded to as making his money by drink, and then giving the results of such traffic to repair the Cathedral of Dublin. It was thousands of pounds. I call such charity robbing Peter to pay Paul! Immense fortunes are made in the *Liquor Traffic*, and I will tell you why; it is all paid for in cash, at least such as the poor people buy; they get credit for clothes, butchers' meat, groceries, etc., while they give the gin-palace keeper *cash;* they never begrudge the price of a glass of gin or beer, they never haggle over *its* price, never once think of doing that; but in the purchase of almost every other article they haggle and begrudge its price. To give you an idea of its profits—there are houses here whose average weekly takings in cash at their bars, is 50*l*., 60*l*., 70*l*., 80*l*., 90*l*., to 150*l*. per week! Nearly all the men of intelligence in it, say it is the curse of the *working classes*. Men whose earnings are, say 20*s*. to 30*s*. per week, spend on the average 3*s*. to 6*s*. per week (some even 10*s*.). It's my mode of living to supply these houses with corks that makes me see so much of the drunkenness; and that is the cause why I never really cared for *my trade*, seeing the misery that was entailed on my fellow men and women by the use of this stuff. Again, a house with a licence to sell spirits, wine, and ale, to be consumed on the premises, is worth two to three times more money than any other class of property. One house here worth nominally 140*l*. sold the other day for 520*l*.; another one worth 200*l*. sold for 800*l*. I know premises with a licence that were sold for 1,300*l*., and then sold again two years after for 1,800*l*.; another place was rented for 50*l*., now rents at 100*l*.—this last is a house used by working men and labourers chiefly! No, I honour men like *Sir W. Trevelyan*, that are teetotalers, or total abstainers, as an example to poor men, and, to prevent his work-people being tempted, will not allow any public-house on his estate. If our land had a few such men it would help the cause. We possess one such a man here, a banker. I feel sorry to say the progress of temperance is not so great as I would like to see it. The only religious body that approaches to your ideas of political economy is Quakerism as taught by George Fox. Carlyle seems deeply tinged with their teachings. *Silence* to them is as valuable as to him. Again, why should people howl and shriek over the law that the Alliance is now trying to carry out in our land called the Permissive Bill? If we had just laws we then would not be so miserable or so much annoyed now and then with cries of Reform and cries of Distress. I send you two pamphlets;—one gives the working man's reasons why he don't go to church; in it you will see a few opinions expressed very much akin to those you have written to me. The other gives an account how it is the poor Indians have died of *Famine*, simply because they have destroyed the very system of Political Economy, or one having some approach to it, that you are now endeavouring to direct the attention of thinkers to in our country. The *Sesame and Lilies* I have read as you requested. I feel now fully the aim and object you have in view in the Letters, but I cannot help directing your attention to that portion where you mention or rather exclaim against the Florentines pulling down their *Ancient Walls* to build a *Boulevard*. That passage is one that would gladden the hearts of all true *Italians*, especially men that love *Italy and Dante!*"

APPENDIX V.

Page 78.—*Abuse of Food.*

PARAGRAPHS cut from 'Manchester Examiner' of March 16, 1867 :—

"A PARISIAN CHARACTER.—A celebrated character has disappeared from the Palais Royal. Réné Lartique was a Swiss, and a man of about sixty. He actually spent the last fifteen years in the Palais Royal—that is to say, he spent the third of his life at dinner. Every morning at ten o'clock he was to be seen going into a restaurant (usually Tissat's), and in a few moments was installed in a corner, which he only quitted about three o'clock in the afternoon, after having drunk at least six or seven bottles of different kinds of wine. He then walked up and down the garden till the clock struck five, when he made his appearance again at the same restaurant, and always at the same place. His second meal, at which he drank quite as much as at the first, invariably lasted till half-past nine. Therefore, he devoted nine hours a day to eating and drinking. His dress was most wretched—his shoes broken, his trousers torn, his paletôt without any lining and patched, his waistcoat without buttons, his hat a rusty red from old age, and the whole surmounted by a dirty white beard. One day he went up to the *comptoir*, and asked the presiding divinity there to allow him to run in debt for one day's dinner. He perceived some hesitation in complying with the request, and immediately called one of the waiters, and desired him to follow him. He went into the office, unbuttoned a certain indispensable garment, and, taking off a broad leather belt, somewhat startled the waiter by displaying two hundred gold pieces, each worth one hundred francs. Taking up one of them, he tossed it to the waiter, and desired him to pay whatever he owed. He never again appeared at that restaurant, and died a few days ago of indigestion."

"Revenge in a Ball-Room.—A distressing event lately took place at Castellaz, a little commune of the Alpes-Maritimes, near Mentone. All the young people of the place being assembled in a dancing-room, one of the young men was seen to fall suddenly to the ground, whilst a young woman, his partner, brandished a poniard, and was preparing to inflict a second blow on him, having already desperately wounded him in the stomach. The author of the crime was at once arrested. She declared her name to be Marie P——, twenty-one years of age, and added that she had acted from a motive of revenge, the young man having led her astray formerly with a promise of marriage, which he had never fulfilled. In the morning of that day she had summoned him to keep his word, and, upon his refusal, had determined on making the dancing-room the scene of her revenge. She was at first locked up in the prison of Mentone, and afterwards sent on to Nice. The young man continues in an alarming state."

APPENDIX VI.

Page 94.—*Regulations of Trade.*

I PRINT portions of two letters of Mr. Dixon's in this place; one referring to our former discussion respecting the sale of votes:—

"57, Nile Street, Sunderland, March 21, 1867.

"I only wish I could write in some tolerable good style, so that I could idealize, or rather realize to folks, the life, and love, and marriage of a working man and his wife. It is in my opinion a working man that really does know what a true wife is, for his every want, his every comfort in life depends on her; and his children's home, their daily lives and future lives, are shaped by her. Napoleon wisely said, 'France needs good mothers more than brave men. Good mothers are the makers or shapers of good and brave men.' I cannot say that these are the words, but it is the import of his speech on the topic. We have a saying amongst us : 'The man may spend and money lend, if his wife be *ought*,'—*i.e.* good wife ;—'but he may work and try to save, but will have *nought*, if his wife be nought,'—*i.e.* bad or thriftless wife.

"Now, since you are intending to treat of the working man's parliament and its duties, I will just throw out a few suggestions of what I consider should be the questions or measures that demand an early enquiry into and debate on. That guilds be established in every town, where masters and men may meet, so as to avoid the temptations of the public-house and *drink*. And then, let it be made law that every lad should serve an apprenticeship of not less than seven years to a trade or art, before he is allowed to be a member of such guild ; also, that all wages be based on a rate of so much *per hour*, and not day, as at present ; and let every man prove his workmanship before such a guild ; and then allow to him such payment per hour as his craft merits. Let there be three grades, and then let there be trials of skill in workmanship every year ; and then, if the workman of the third grade prove that he has made progress in his craft, reward him accordingly. Then, before a lad is put to any trade, why not see what he is naturally fitted for ? Combe's book, entitled *The Constitution of Man*, throws a good deal of truth on to these matters. Now, here are two branches of the science of life that, so far, have never once been given trial of in this way. We certainly use them after a *crime* has been committed, but not till then.

"Next to that, cash payment for all and everything needed in life. *Credit is a curse* to him that gives it, and that takes it. He that lives by credit lives in general carelessly. If there was no credit, people then would have to live on what they earned! Then, after that, the Statute of Limitations of Fortune you propose. By the hour system, not a single man *need be idle;* it would give employment to all, and even two hours per day would realize more to a man than *breaking stones.* Thus you would make every one self-dependent—also no fear of being out of work altogether. Then let there be a Government fund for all the savings of the working man. I am afraid you will think this a wild, discursive sort of a letter.

"Yours truly,
"THOMAS DIXON."

"I have read your references to the *Times* on 'Bribery.' Well, that has long been my own opinion; they simply have a vote to sell, and sell it the same way as they sell potatoes, or a coat, or any other saleable article. Voters generally say, 'What does this gentleman want in Parliament? Why, to help himself and his family or friends; he does not spend all the money he spends over his election for pure good of his country! No: it's to benefit his pocket, to be sure. Why should I not make a penny with my vote, as well as he does with his in Parliament?' I think that if the system of canvassing or election agents were done away with, and all personal canvassing for votes entirely abolished, it would help to put down bribery. Let each gentleman send to the electors his political opinions in a circular, and then let papers be sent, or cards, to each elector, and then let them go and record their votes in the same way they do for a councillor in the Corporation. It would save a great deal of expense, and prevent those scenes of drunkenness so common in our towns during elections. *Bewick's opinions* of these matters are quite to the purpose, I think (*see page* 201 *of Memoir*). Again, respecting the Paris matter referred to in your last letter, I have read it. Does it not manifest plainly enough that Europeans are also in a measure possessed with that same *demoniacal spirit like the Japanese?*"

APPENDIX VII.

THE following letter did not form part of the series written to Mr. Dixon; but is perhaps worth reprinting. I have not the date of the number of the *Gazette* in which it appeared, but it was during the tailors' strike in London.

"'To the Editor of the *Pall Mall Gazette*.

"Sir,—

"In your yesterday's article on strikes you have very neatly and tersely expressed the primal fallacy of modern political economy—to wit, that 'the value of any piece of labour cannot be defined'—and that 'all that can be ascertained is simply whether any man can be got to do it for a certain sum.' Now, sir, the 'value' of any piece of labour, that is to say, the quantity of food and air which will enable a man to perform it without losing actually any of his flesh or his nervous energy, is as absolutely fixed a quantity as the weight of powder necessary to carry a given ball a given distance. And within limits varying by exceedingly minor and unimportant circumstances, it is an ascertainable quantity. I told the public this five years ago—and under pardon of your politico-economical contributors—it is not a 'sentimental,' but a chemical fact.

"Let any half-dozen of recognised London physicians state in precise terms the quantity and kind of food, and space of lodging, they consider approximately necessary for the healthy life of a labourer in any given manufacture, and the number of hours he may, without shortening his life, work at such business daily if so sustained.

"And let all masters be bound to give their men a choice between an order for that quantity of food and lodging, or such wages as the market may offer for that number of hours' work.

"Proper laws for the maintenance of families would require further concession—but, in the outset, let but *this* law of wages be established, and if then we have any more strikes you may denounce them without one word of remonstrance either from sense or sensibility.

"I am, Sir,
"Your obedient servant,
"JOHN RUSKIN."

THE END.

Printed by Hazell, Watson, & Viney, Ld., London and Aylesbury.

www.ingramcontent.com/pod-product-compliance
Lightning Source LLC
Chambersburg PA
CBHW020808230426
43666CB00007B/908